THE Unexplained

The UFO Casebook

Startling cases and astonishing photographs of encounters with flying saucers

Editor: Peter Brookesmith

Acknowledgements
Photographs were supplied by ATV Network, H. Cowin, Count Down, Mary Evans Picture Library, Flying Saucer Review, Foto Efe, Fortean Picture Library, French Government Tourist Office, Gente y la Actualidad, Ground Saucer Watch, Mike Hooks, Robert Hunt Picture Library, Anwar Hussein, P.R. Marsh, Martin Aircraft Co., NASA, Photri, Popperfoto, Rex Features, Space Frontiers, Neville Spearman Ltd, Michael Taylor, UPI, USAF, P. Warrington, ZEFA.

Consultants:
Professor A J Ellinson
Dr J Allen Hynek
Brian Inglis
Colin Wilson

First published in the United Kingdom by
Orbis Publishing Limited 1984
Reprinted 1989 by Macdonald & Co (Publishers) Ltd
Reprinted under Black Cat imprint 1990

Material in this publication previously appeared in the weekly partwork *The Unexplained* © 1980-83

Macdonald & Co (Publishers) Ltd
Orbit House, 1 New Fetter Lane,
London EC4A 1AR

a member of Maxwell Macmillan Pergamon Publishing Corporation

ISBN 0-7481-0302 3

Printed and bound in Hungary

Contents

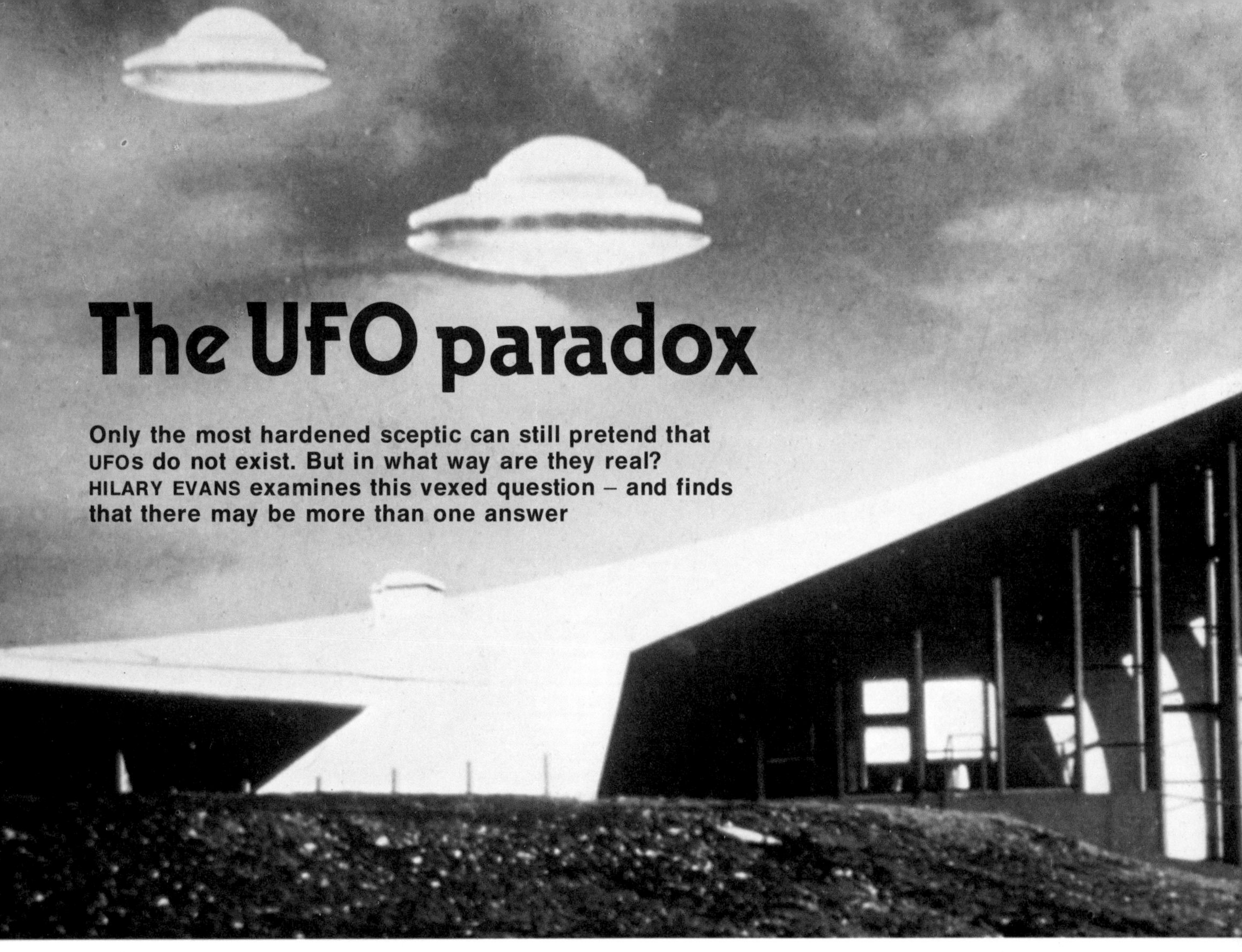

The UFO paradox

Only the most hardened sceptic can still pretend that UFOs do not exist. But in what way are they real? HILARY EVANS examines this vexed question – and finds that there may be more than one answer

'THEY FLEW LIKE A SAUCER would if you skipped it across the water.' This is how, on 24 June 1947, American airman Kenneth Arnold, an experienced pilot, described some unusual flying craft he had seen over the mountains of America's west coast. Newspapermen applied his phrase to the craft themselves, and the misleading label 'flying saucer' has followed the UFO ever since, like a tin can tied to a cat's tail.

This fanciful name has deepened the reluctance of professional scientists to take the UFO seriously. Only a few have taken the trouble to investigate this bizarre phenomenon, which surely qualifies as the strangest of our time. Even that phrase, 'of our time', is a subject of controversy: many people claim that the UFO has been with mankind throughout history. But the evidence they offer is meagre and their case far from proven. There seems little doubt that our earliest ancestors were considerably more advanced than has generally been supposed, but that is a long way from the theory that our planet was long ago visited by extraterrestrial voyagers.

Whether or not UFOs existed in the past, there is no doubt that UFO sightings have proliferated in astonishing numbers over the past 30 years. This fact seems to be in some way linked with man's first steps towards exploring space, and this connection is undoubtedly an important clue in trying to explain the UFO.

Estimates of the total number of UFO sightings vary so widely as to be meaningless; more helpful figures are provided by the catalogues of reported sightings prepared by individual investigative organisations. Recently a French team catalogued more than 600 encounter cases in France alone, each vouched for by responsible investigators; how many more were not reported or investigated? In the early 1970s UFO investigators made lists of all reported landing cases for particular countries: 923 were recorded in the United States, 200 in Spain.

Are UFOs real in the sense that, say, spacecraft are real? The surest proof would be actually to get hold of one, and there are persistent rumours that certain governments, notably that of the United States, have indeed obtained a UFO, which is kept in total secrecy. However this remains mere conjecture, despite the sworn affidavits of alleged witnesses. Indeed, the whole matter of governmental involvement – or the lack of it – is a further and fascinating aspect of the UFO controversy.

In the absence of a real UFO that we can touch and examine, there is a great deal of evidence of the phenomenon in the form of a

Above: Kenneth Arnold's book, first published in 1952, was the first full study of UFOs. Arnold began collecting accounts of UFO sightings after he saw several disc-shaped objects in the sky in June 1947

mass of photographs and a handful of movies. The majority are undoubtedly fakes. Those with good credentials are so blurred, so distant or so ambiguous that they simply add a further dimension to the problem: why, if UFOs exist, and in an age when many people carry cameras with them most of the time, have we not obtained better photographic evidence?

Perhaps the strongest evidence we have is from the effects caused by UFOs on surrounding objects, particularly machinery. In November 1967 a truck and a car approaching each other on a Hampshire road in the early hours of the morning simultaneously suffered engine failure when a large egg-shaped object crossed the road between them. The police, and subsequently the Ministry of Defence, investigated the incident, but no official explanation was ever issued. Such a case may leave investigators puzzled, but it makes one thing certain: if they can cause physical effects, UFOs must be physically real.

If they are physical objects, UFOs must originate from somewhere. When the first UFOs of the current era were seen, back in the 1940s, it was assumed they came from somewhere on Earth. The Americans suspected they were a Russian secret device, perhaps developed using the expertise of German scientists captured at the end of the Second World War.

But as more reports came in it became clear that no nation on Earth could be responsible. Nor was there sufficient evidence to support other ingenious theories – that they came from the Himalayas, long a favoured source of secret wisdom, or Antarctica, where unexplored tracts of land and climatic anomalies provide a shaky foundation for speculation. Instead, ufologists began to look beyond the Earth, encouraged by the fact that our own space exploration programme was just beginning. We were starting to take an active interest in worlds beyond, and it seemed reasonable that other civilizations might have a similar interest in us.

However, although the number of potential sources of life in the Universe is virtually infinite, the probability of any civilisation being at a stage of development appropriate for space travel is very small. The fact that no solid evidence has been found for the extraterrestrial hypothesis is discouraging. Although it is the best available explanation, it remains no more than speculation.

Right: this photograph was taken at Taormina, Sicily, in 1954. Sceptics claim the 'objects' are nothing more than lenticular clouds, or even the result of lens flare

Below: a shot taken from Skylab III in 1973. The object rotated for several minutes before disappearing. UFOs have been reported by almost all astronauts

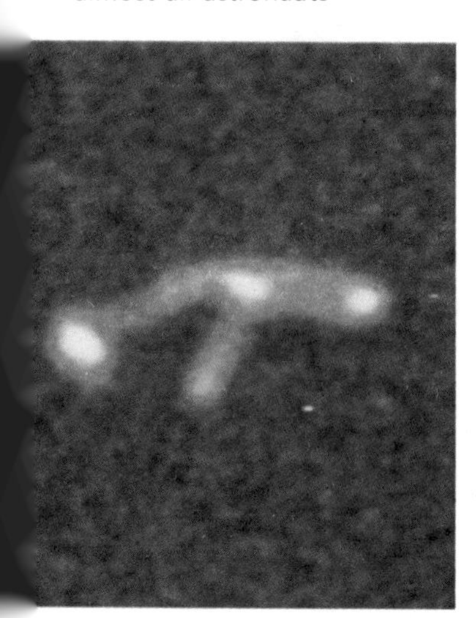

Messages from outer space?

Today it is recognised that the UFO poses a problem not only for the astronomer and the engineer, but also for the behavioural scientist. The psychologist confirms that an individual's response to a sighting is conditioned by his psychological make-up, while the sociologist places such responses in a wider social context and relates them to cultural patterns. The anthropologist detects parallels with myth and traditional belief, while the parapsychologist notes how frequently sightings are accompanied by such psychic manifestations as precognition and poltergeist phenomena.

This is particularly true of 'encounter' cases in which the observer claims to have had actual meetings with UFO occupants. The entities are generally described as extraterrestrial aliens, often ambassadors from an inter-galactic power; their purpose is to examine human beings, to warn us of misuse of resources and to bring reassuring messages from some cosmic brotherhood. With only one or two such cases on record they could be dismissed as fantasy, but there are hundreds of such cases on file.

If a single one of these cases could be shown to be based on fact, the UFO problem would be established on solid foundations and serious scientific interest assured. But in every instance it remains an open question whether the incident actually occurred or is simply a fabrication – deliberate, unconscious, or perhaps induced by some external force. Hypotheses range from brainwashing by extraterrestrial invaders, to deliberate invention by the CIA.

Almost certainly, UFOs exist on both the physical and the psychological level. Somehow we have got to recognise that, although they are real, they are not what they seem. This is the paradox that lies at the heart of the UFO mystery, which we examine in the classic UFO case histories that follow.

Strange encounters of many kinds

Unidentified flying objects have intrigued the world for decades, but objective reports by experienced investigators rarely reach the mass media. CHARLES BOWEN examines our collection of carefully authenticated cases

ESTABLISHED SCIENCE has always tended to view the UFO phenomenon with scepticism. In his book, *The UFO experience*, Dr J. Allen Hynek, who was astronomical consultant to Project Blue Book (the US Air Force investigation into UFOs), tells the story of an event at an evening reception held in 1968 in Victoria, British Columbia, at which a number of astronomers were present. During the evening it was announced that strange lights – possibly UFOs – had been spotted outside. Dr Hynek continues: 'The news was met by casual banter and the giggling sound that often accompanies an embarrassing situation.' And, he reports, not a single astronomer went outside to look.

Even Project Blue Book attempted to explain away every reported sighting in terms of conventional science. It soon began to earn itself a bad name because many of its explanations were impossible to believe. In 1966 the US Air Force set up a two-year research project – to investigate, in effect, its own investigations!

The Condon Report, as it was unofficially known, was published in 1969 and stated, broadly, that since nothing valuable to science had come out of the study of UFOs, further research was not justified. This conclusion was reached despite the fact that about one in three of the 87 case histories studied by the commission remained unexplained in the report. After this the US Air Force relinquished responsibility for the monitoring of UFO reports and Project Blue Book was disbanded in December 1969. Since 1969 research has been largely left to private organisations, such as Ground Saucer Watch and Project Starlight International in the USA, and UFOIN (UFO Investigators' Network and BUFORA (British UFO Research Association) in Britain.

From UFO reports made over the past 30 years it has been observed that they occur in distinct waves, often called 'flaps'. The flaps of 1954 and 1965, when reports reached vast numbers, were particularly interesting. Featured below are two incidents from the 1954 flap. The third incident we describe, at Socorro, New Mexico, belongs to the smaller flap of 1964; it is a classic early example of an encounter involving humanoids.

What kind of sighting?

Astronomer Dr J. Allen Hynek, Director of the Centre for UFO Studies, USA. Dr Hynek has spent many years in applying the techniques of science to the study of UFOs

Dr J. Allen Hynek, while acting as a consultant to Project Blue Book, developed a system of classification of UFO 'types' which has become standard. He divided UFO reports according to the distance, greater or less than 500 feet (150 metres), at which the UFO was observed, and subdivided each of these two sections into three, giving six categories altogether.

The commonest sightings are of the 'distant' type.

Nocturnal lights Strange lights seen at a distance in the night sky, often with unusual features such as variations in the intensity of light or colour and sudden, remarkable changes of speed and direction of movement.

Daylight discs Distant objects seen against the sky during the daytime. The shapes vary considerably: cigars, spheres, eggs, ovals and pinpoints as well as discs are often reported.

Radar-visuals Distant UFOs recorded simultaneously on radar and visually with good agreement between the two reports. Dr Hynek excluded 'sightings' made solely by radar since false traces can result from a number of natural factors such as ground scatter – the signal is reflected from high ground – temperature inversions and even thick banks of cloud or flocks of birds. Radar-visual sightings are the most important category of UFO reports as they give independent instrumental evidence of the sighting; unfortunately, they are very rare.

Reports of UFOs seen at close range are the most interesting and often spectacular; these are the famous 'close encounters'.

Close encounters of the first kind Simple observations of phenomena where there is no physical interaction between the phenomena and the environment.

Close encounters of the second kind Similar to the first kind except that physical effects on both animate and inanimate matter are observed. Vegetation may be scorched or flattened, tree branches broken, animals frightened or car headlights, engines and radios doused. In cases of electrical failure the equipment usually begins to work normally again once the UFO has disappeared.

Close encounters of the third kind 'Occupants' are reported in or around the UFO. Dr Hynek generally ruled out so-called 'contactee' cases in which the reporter claimed to have had intelligent communication with the 'occupants', arguing that such reports were almost invariably made by pseudo-religious fanatics and never by 'ostensibly sensible, rational and reputable persons.' But even these cases occasionally have to be taken seriously by scientists.

'We are not alone'

Radar-visual: Atlantic Ocean off Labrador, 29 June 1954

The UFO seen by Captain James Howard and the crew and passengers of BOAC Stratocruiser *Centaurus* on 29 June 1954 was not a saucer or a disc; it was, astonishingly, a shape that kept changing shape. The airliner had taken off from Idlewild, New York, bound for Newfoundland before making the Atlantic crossing to Shannon, then London.

The airliner was making its way steadily northeastwards when the radio crackled an order from ground control to 'hold' – a manoeuvre adopted when there is a hazard ahead. After half an hour's circling the skipper advised control that if he couldn't proceed he would have to return to Idlewild, as his fuel was low. After some delay permission was given to proceed and *Centaurus* went on automatic pilot at 19,000 feet (6000 metres), just below a broken layer of cloud and with a solid mass of cloud beneath it at 200 feet (60 metres). After some 20 minutes a glint of light suddenly caught Captain Howard's eye. On the port side of the aircraft he saw a large object of metallic appearance emerge from a gap in the clouds. Moving around this main shape were six much smaller objects, not unlike a screen of small destroyers escorting an enormous aircraft carrier.

A bizarre aspect of this remarkable apparition was that it seemed to be changing shape all the time. Captain Howard sketched on his knee pad the different forms he saw: they were a 'delta wing', a telephone handset, a pear. He has since said that, with its continual changes in shape, the object reminded him of a swarm of bees in flight. It was an estimated 4 miles (6 kilometres) from *Centaurus* and it maintained that position.

When Captain Howard turned to speak to his first officer, Lee Boyd, he found him already out of his seat, standing to watch the display. Captain Howard called up control:

'We are not alone.'

'We know.'

'What is it?'

'We don't know, but we've scrambled a Sabre from Goose Bay to investigate.'

'Good. Give me his frequency and I'll vector him in.'

A few minutes later the captain was in touch with the pilot of the Sabre jet fighter who, once he was in range, announced he had two images on his radar scope – one for *Centaurus* and the other, presumably, for the UFO. Then the unexpected happened: the six small objects manoeuvred into single file, bore down on the main object and appeared to merge into one end of it. Thereafter the size of the large UFO began to diminish until the Sabre's pilot announced he was overhead, at which point the object finally disappeared from the radar scope '. . . like a TV picture going off'.

Since about 1953, airline pilots have been required not to disclose to the public information about UFO sightings. In the case of *Centaurus*, however, many of the passengers had watched the display with amazement and the incident received wide press coverage. Researchers were fortunate in this, for this sighting falls into the important category of radar/visual cases. In this instance two separate radar sets were involved (at control and in the Sabre) plus visual observation by experienced pilots, air crew and some 30 or more passengers – only one of whom had a camera, and he was asleep!

'Luminous, silent and eerily still'

Nocturnal lights: Vernon, France, 23 August 1954

Vernon lies on the River Seine some 50 miles (80 kilometres) downstream from Paris; it is the point at which the Allied forces first crossed the river in pursuit of the German armies in 1944. Ten years later, and barely eight weeks after the Idlewild affair, the town was the scene of another significant event, which was witnessed by four people but received little attention in the press.

The sky was clear at 1 a.m. on 23 August 1954, with the moon in its third quarter and due to appear later that night and give only a faint light. M. Bernard Miserey had just returned home and was closing his garage door when he saw a giant cigar-shaped object hanging vertically over the north bank of the river about 300 yards (275 metres) from him. This object, which he estimated to be some 300 feet (90 metres) long, was luminous, silent and eerily still. While the witness gaped at the phenomenon, a horizontal, disc-shaped object dropped from the bottom of the giant 'cigar', halted its free-fall, wobbled, turned a luminous red with a brilliant white halo and shot towards M. Miserey, passing silently over his house heading south-west.

This remarkable happening was repeated three times, then, after an interval, a fifth disc dropped almost to the level of the river bank before wobbling and disappearing at great speed to the north. While this last manoeuvre was under way the glow of the giant cigar began to fade and soon it was lost in darkness.

M. Miserey reported the incident to the police and was informed that two policemen on their rounds had also observed the happenings, as had an army engineer who was driving on Route Nationale 181 south-west of the town.

What was the meaning of the apparition M. Miserey saw? Was the large cigar-shaped object the 'carrier' of the smaller ones? Other UFO sightings have led many people to think this may be the case – including the Idlewild incident. The significant difference is that, whereas at Idlewild the smaller objects were assimilated by the larger one, at Vernon the small objects were ejected. But no conclusive evidence exists to establish what these objects in the sky actually are.

'Humanoids . . . and strange insignia'

Close encounter of the third kind: Socorro, New Mexico, USA, 24 April 1964

At about 5.50 p.m. on 24 April 1964 Patrolman Lonnie Zamora of the Police Department in Socorro, New Mexico, was alone in his Pontiac giving chase to a speeding motorist who was heading out of town. Suddenly he heard a roar and at the same time saw a 'flame' in the sky, bluish and orange and strangely static as it descended some distance away. Fearful that a nearby dynamite shack might blow up, the patrolman gave up chasing the motorist and headed off over rough ground towards the point where the flame had come down.

After three attempts he forced his car to the top of a ridge and drove slowly westwards. He stopped when, suddenly, he saw a shiny, aluminium-like object below him, about 150–200 yards (140–185 metres) south of his position. Zamora said it looked like a car on end, perhaps 'turned over by some kids'. Then he saw two humanoid figures in white 'coveralls' close to the object. He estimated later that they were about 4 feet (1.2 metres) tall. One of them looked straight at him and seemed to jump. Zamora was wearing clip-on sunglasses over his prescription spectacles and couldn't distinguish any features or headgear at that distance.

The patrolman now accelerated thinking that, whoever the strangers were, they might be in need of help. The shape he'd seen was a sort of vertical oval, and looking down he could see it was supported on girderlike legs. When the terrain became too rough for the car to go any further he radioed his headquarters to say that he was near the scene of a possible accident and would proceed on foot.

As Zamora left the car he heard two or three loud thumps, like someone hammering or slamming a door. These thumps were a second or two apart. When he was about 50 paces from the object there was a loud roar, which rose gradually in pitch. The humanoid figures were nowhere to be seen. At the same time he could see a blue and orange flame rise from the ground leaving a cloud of dust. Zamora beat a hasty retreat towards his car

Below: Patrolman Lonnie Zamora whose close encounter is one of the best authenticated cases on record

and as he reached it turned to see the oval shape, now horizontal, rising towards the level of the car. Frightened by the continuing roar, he ran on and dived for shelter over the edge of the ridge. When he realised the noise had ceased he raised his head from his hands and saw the UFO still in the air and moving away from him about 15 feet (4.5 metres) above the ground. It safely cleared the dynamite shack and continued to rise gradually, watched by the policeman, who was retracing his steps to the car. As he called up the radio officer he watched it accelerate away to clear a mountain range and disappear.

Zamora had seen a kind of strange insignia about 18 inches (45 centimetres) high on the side of the object and while he was waiting for his sergeant to arrive he decided to make a sketch of it.

Sergeant Sam Chavez was soon on the scene. Had he not taken a wrong turning he would have arrived in time to see the craft.

'What's the matter, Lonnie?' he asked. 'You look like you've seen the devil.'

'Maybe I have,' replied Zamora.

Zamora pointed out to Sergeant Chavez the fire that was still burning in the brush where the UFO had stood. When they descended to the site they found four separate burn marks and four depressions – all of similar shape – made, they assumed, by the legs of the landing gear. On three of the marks the dense soil had been pushed down about 2 inches (50 millimetres) and dirt had been squeezed up at the sides. The fourth pad mark, less well defined, was only 1 inch (25 millimetres) deep. When engineer W. T. Powers investigated the case he estimated that the force that produced the marks was 'equivalent to a gentle settling of at least a ton on each mark!' He also pointed out an interesting fact about the positions of the marks. Measurements show that the diagonals of a quadrilateral intersect at right angles, then the midpoints of the sides all lie on the circumference of a circle. Mr Powers noted that one of the burn marks occurred on the intersection of the diagonals and speculated that, assuming the linkage among the legs was flexible, this would mean the burn was immediately below the centre of gravity of the craft and might indicate the position of the blue and orange flame seen by Patrolman Zamora. Four small round marks were found within the quadrilateral on the side farthest from where Patrolman Zamora had stood; these were described as 'footprints'.

The Socorro incident was widely reported in the press and generated immense excitement throughout the world. The US Air Force's Project Blue Book usually ruled out UFO sightings with only one witness, but at Socorro Patrolman Zamora's story was so plausible that it was decided to carry out intensive on-the-spot investigations. This was one case in which Project Blue Book was forced to admit defeat: the apparition could not be explained as any known device or phenomenon. Dr J. Allen Hynek admitted that he was more puzzled after completing the investigation than when he had arrived in Socorro. He commented, 'Maybe there *is* a simple, natural explanation for the Socorro incident, but having made a complete study of the events, I do not think so.'

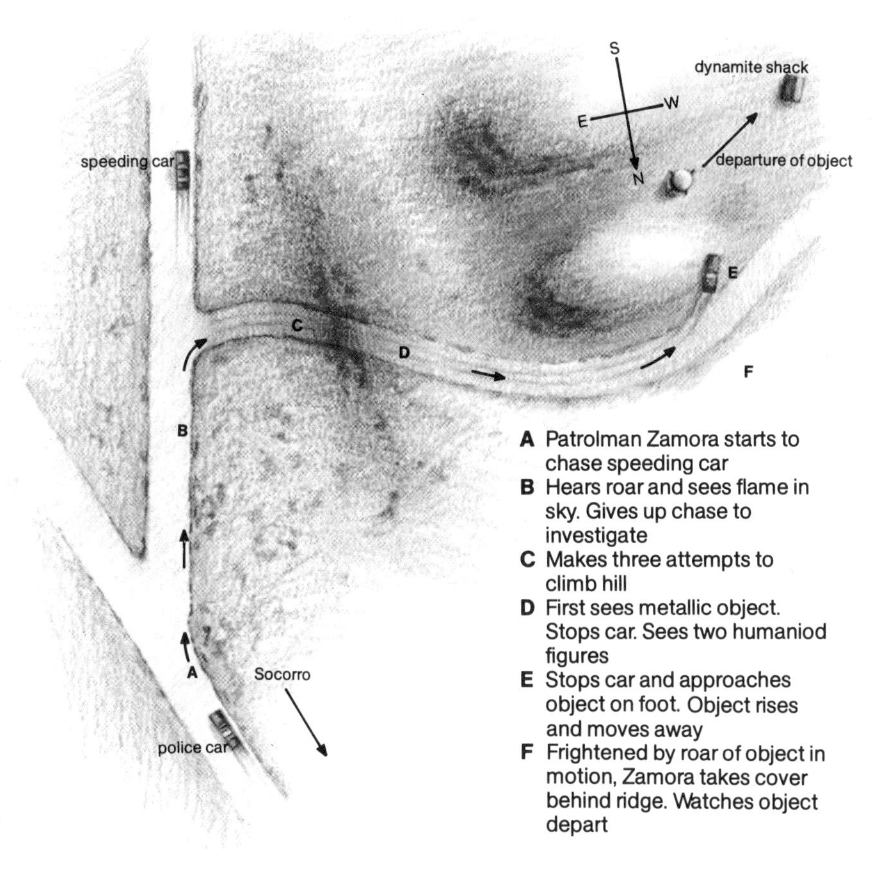

A Patrolman Zamora starts to chase speeding car
B Hears roar and sees flame in sky. Gives up chase to investigate
C Makes three attempts to climb hill
D First sees metallic object. Stops car. Sees two humaniod figures
E Stops car and approaches object on foot. Object rises and moves away
F Frightened by roar of object in motion, Zamora takes cover behind ridge. Watches object depart

Below: one of the four impressions left by the UFO which landed at Sorocco, New Mexico on 24 April 1964. An engineer said pressure of 1 ton would have been needed to make the holes

him for 90 minutes.

Dr J. Allen Hynek is very wary of all so-called 'contactee' cases. And Allen Hendry, author of *The UFO handbook*, points out a suspicious feature of 'contactee' reports: until the late 1950s, when it was still believed that planets in our solar system were likely to be able to support intelligent life, most of the reported visitors came from Mars, Jupiter and Venus – but once scientists had proved that this was unlikely, the visitors began to hail from planets outside our own solar system.

Paul Villa's photographs have been subjected to very detailed analysis by Ground Saucer Watch Inc., a UFO organization in Phoenix, Arizona. Using advanced computer techniques, they can establish the exact shape of an alleged UFO, its distance from the camera, and even estimate its true size. Paul Villa's photographs failed GSW's tests: comparison between the photographic images of the UFOs and surrounding objects revealed that the alleged UFOs were in fact small objects seen at close range – not, as Villa had claimed, large ones at a distance. GSW have been known to be wrong – but ufologists the world over agree that Villa's pictures are just too *good* to be true!

THE BEST UFO pictures usually turn out to be hoaxes; pictures of well-documented sightings are usually blurs on under- or over-exposed film.

These spectacular photographs, taken by Paul Villa in Albuquerque, New Mexico, are almost certainly fakes. The top photograph shows an object Villa claims to have seen on 18 April 1965; its three occupants, he says, talked to him. The other two pictures are views of a UFO he photographed on 16 June 1963. It contained nine beings from the constellation of Coma Berenices, who conversed with him for 90 minutes.

Right: at about 6 p.m. on 19 November 1974, Christophe Fernandez, aged 16, was alone at home near Uzès in southern France. Suddenly he noticed a bright light outside. Forty yards (35 metres) from the house was a luminous sphere 2.5 yards (2.2 metres) wide. It was standing still on the ground or just above it.

Christophe could hear a faint 'glug-glug' sound like a bottle being emptied. On the surface of the sphere three circular shapes were moving about. Trembling, Christophe managed to photograph them.

Next, the globe rose slowly to a height of 5 or 6 yards (4 or 5 metres). A dazzlingly bright cylinder, about 1 yard (1 metre) long emerged from the underside of the sphere. Then the UFO suddenly shot upwards and out of sight

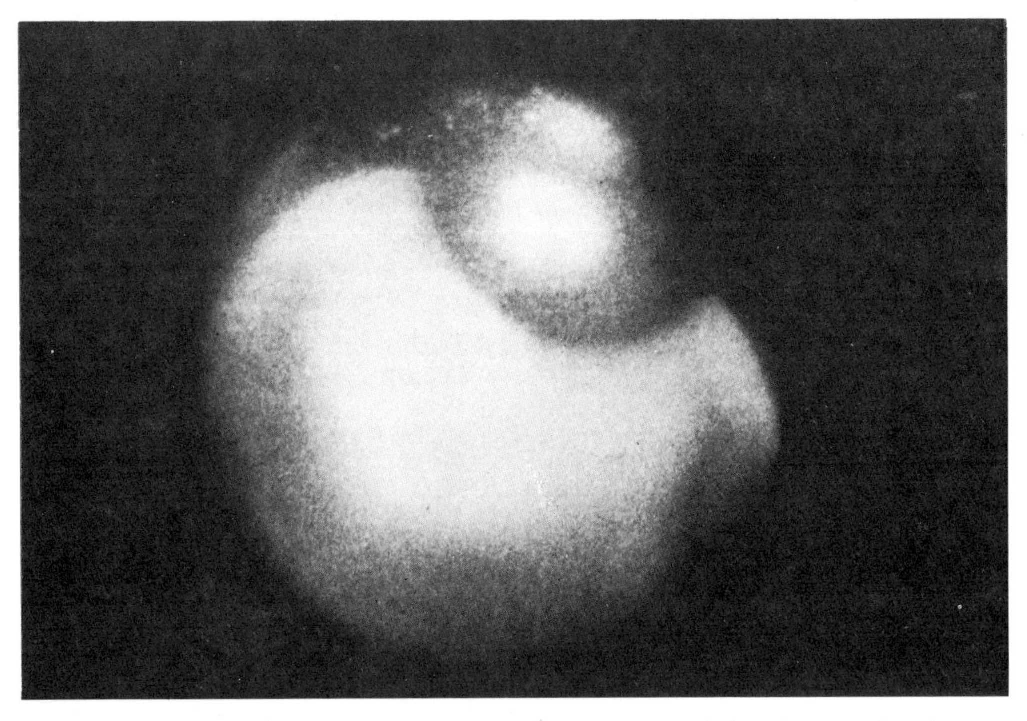

Left: 15-year-old Stephen Pratt and his mother were returning from a visit to the local fish-and-chip shop to their home in Conisbrough, Yorkshire, on the evening of 28 March 1966. At about 8.30 p.m. they saw an orange-coloured light in the twilit sky.

The light, they said, was 'throbbing'. Stephen went indoors to fetch his Instamatic camera, which was loaded with black and white film and set for 'cloudy'. Stephen took one shot of the light, which was travelling westwards.

Stephen claimed to have watched the light for 10 minutes – a long time for a UFO sighting. The film was taken to a local chemist's shop for processing, but when the negatives and prints were collected it was discovered that no print had been made of the 'UFO' negative.

Later Stephen sent his film to Granada TV asking them if they could explain the strange objects on the negative. Granada made the first prints and broadcast the photograph on 12 April 1966.

The negative did not appear to have been tampered with. The strangest feature of the story, however, is that, although Stephen told investigators he had seen only one light, the photograph shows three objects – and they appear to be solid, shaped like flying saucers, not lights.

The men from Mars

WHEN PATROLMAN Lonnie Zamora saw two small humanoids beside a UFO near Socorro, New Mexico, at about 6.50 p.m. on 24 April 1964 (previous case), he was not the first American that day to experience such an encounter. Several hundred miles away, a dairy farmer of Newark Valley, New York State, had not only seen two ufonauts emerge from their craft at about 10.00 a.m., but also claimed he had conversed with them.

'We have spoken to people before'

Close encounter of the third kind: Newark Valley, New York State, USA, 24 April 1964

At about 10.00 a.m. on 24 April 1964, farmer Gary Wilcox of Newark Valley, Tioga County, was using his manure spreader in a field to the east of his farmhouse. It was a clear, sunny day, and the ground was dry.

The field sloped up a hill, at the top of which stood an old abandoned refrigerator, half hidden by trees. Suddenly Gary saw a glint of something shining. At first he thought it was the refrigerator, but it soon dawned on him that the shining object was between him and the fridge. His curiosity aroused, Gary drove the tractor, with spreader in tow, up the slope to the top of the hill – about 800 yards (730 metres) from where he had first seen the thing.

With about 100 yards (90 metres) still to go, it occurred to him that he might be looking at a fuel tank from the wing of an aeroplane; he stopped the tractor and walked over towards the object. Then he realised that the thing was off the ground, presumably hovering, for he could not see any 'undercarriage'. As he drew closer to it he could see that it was 'bigger than a car in length . . . shaped something like an egg . . . no seams or rivets. . . .' He estimated later that it was 20 feet (6 metres) long, 4 feet (1.2 metres) high and 15 feet (4.5 metres) wide. He 'thumped it and kicked it . . . it felt like metallic canvas.'

While Gary was carrying out this rough examination, two 4 feet (1.2 metre) tall 'men' came out from under the object, each carrying a tray about 1 foot (30 centimetres) square, 'filled with alfalfa, with roots, soil, leaves and brush'. They walked towards Gary and stopped a couple of yards away.

The farmer said that at first he thought 'it was some kind of a trick . . . a sort of candid camera gag', and he laughed. Amusement turned to surprise when he heard one of the beings speak: 'Don't be alarmed, we have spoken to people before.'

The voice did not sound like one Gary could find words to describe; he could understand what the being said, yet could not tell whether it was speaking in English or not.

Gary said the little 'men' were standing one behind the other. They wore white, metallic-looking overalls without seams, stitching or pockets, and no features of their

bodies were visible. They had arms and legs, but he could not see hands or feet. When the creatures raised their arms, he could see wrinkles where the elbows would be. The farmer could not see faces – eyes, ears, noses, mouths or hair. The voice that addressed him seemed to be coming 'from about them rather than from either of them'.

The conversation continued: 'We are from what you know as the planet Mars.' They asked Gary what he was doing; when he explained, they showed great interest in manure and, when he told them about it, in artificial fertiliser too. Gary said he would get them a bag of fertiliser, whereupon they told him they were 'travelling this hemisphere'. When Gary asked if he should go, the 'spokesman' added that they could only come to Earth every two years, and included a warning that people should not be sent out into space. It seems that Gary asked if he could go back with them, but his request was declined because of the thinness of their atmosphere. The ufonauts also mentioned that astronauts John Glenn and Virgil ('Gus') Grissom, and two Russian cosmonauts, would die within a year, due to exposure in space.

Further revelations were that they were learning about our organic materials because of the 'rocky structure of Mars', and that they did not fly near our cities because the fumes and air pollution affected the flight of their spacecraft.

Gary Wilcox said that no attempt was made to harm him, and that they carried no visible weapons. He also said that their voices stayed at the same pitch throughout, and that they did most of the talking. Then, with a warning that Gary should not mention the encounter, the two mysterious humanoids walked back under their ship, ducking down as they went, and disappeared. The craft made a noise like a car engine idling, then took off gently towards the north, with no blasting, no heat, and no more noise.

The farmer drove home, telephoned his mother and told her what had happened. He then milked his cows, did a few other jobs, and, at 4.30 p.m., he drove up the hill with a bag of fertiliser, which he left at the site of the landing. The next morning, it was gone.

News of the incident spread, and reached the ears of a neighbour, Miss Priscilla Baldwin, who interviewed Gary, alerted the local newspaper, and reported the matter to the Tioga County sheriff. The police investigation was carried out on 1 May 1964, and Gary made a statement to Sheriff Paul J. Taylor and Officer George Williams.

In 1968 a well-known psychiatrist, Berthold Eric Schwarz MD, visited the area and conducted a thorough investigation of the case, with psychiatric study of the witness. In addition Dr Schwarz interviewed many of the farmer's family, friends and neighbours

and, from all of these interviews and the psychiatric examination, it appears that Gary Wilson is a very normal, 'truthful person with no emotional illness, and that his experience was "real" even though the interpretation of his encounter is a complicated and uncertain matter.' In his report, prepared exclusively for *Flying Saucer Review*, Dr Schwarz revealed that Gary had never had any other UFO experiences, either before or since his encounter on 24 April 1964.

As for the alleged prophecy, this was not fulfilled as stated. But on 27 January 1967 Virgil Grissom, together with Ed White and Roger Chaffee, died in a fire in an Apollo spacecraft that was being tested at Cape Kennedy. And on 23 April 1967, three years almost to the day after Gary Wilcox's encounter, the Russian Vladimir Komarov was killed when his capsule parachutes failed to open after re-entry into the atmosphere.

This spinning, luminous sphere was filmed by a New Zealand television crew on the night of 30 December 1978. The crew made two flights, looking for UFOs, on the same night – and, incredibly, saw them both times

Tantalising evidence: The New Zealand UFO film

LATE IN THE EVENING of 30 December 1978 an Argosy freight plane set off from Wellington, New Zealand. Its skipper was Captain Bill Startup, who had 23 years' flying experience behind him, and the co-pilot was Bob Guard. On board was an Australian TV crew from Channel 0-10 Network: reporter Quentin Fogarty, cameraman David Crockett and his wife, sound recordist Ngaire Crockett. Their purpose was to try to film UFOs, for there had been reports of 'unknowns' during the preceding weeks in the region of Cook Strait, which separates New Zealand's North and South Islands. They were spectacularly successful in the quest. So successful that, after the story had appeared in hundreds of newspapers and clips from the films had been shown repeatedly on television around the world – the BBC, for instance, gave it pride of place on the main evening news – critics and droves of debunkers lined up to try to explain what the television crew had seen, in terms ranging from the sublimely astronomical to the ridiculously absurd.

'Bright lights over the ocean'

Radar-visual: Blenheim, New Zealand, 30 December 1978

The Argosy had crossed Cook Strait and was flying over the Pacific Ocean off the north-east coast of South Island when the excitement began. The television crew was down by the loading bay filming 'intros' with Quentin Fogarty when Captain Startup called over the intercom for them to hurry to the flight deck; the pilots had seen some strange objects in the sky. According to Dave Crockett, they had already checked with Wellington air traffic control for radar confirmation of their visual sighting.

Quentin Fogarty stated that when he reached the flight deck he saw a row of five bright lights. Large and brilliant, although a long way off, they were seen to pulsate, growing from pinpoint size to the size of a large balloon full of glowing light. The sequence was repeated, the objects appearing above the street lights of the town of Kaikoura, but between the aircraft and the ground.

Dave Crockett, who was wearing headphones, received a call from Wellington control warning the pilots that an unknown target was following the Argosy. Captain Startup put his plane into a 360-degree turn to look for the unidentified object but the passengers and crew saw nothing. Control however, was insistent: 'Sierra Alpha Eagle . . . you have a target in formation with you . . . target has increased in size.' This time lights were seen outside the plane, but because of interference from the navigation lights of the plane, Crockett was unable to film. So First Officer Bob Guard switched off the navigation lights – and everyone saw a big, bright light. The plane was now back on automatic pilot, so Bob Guard gave up his seat for Crockett, who obtained a clear shot

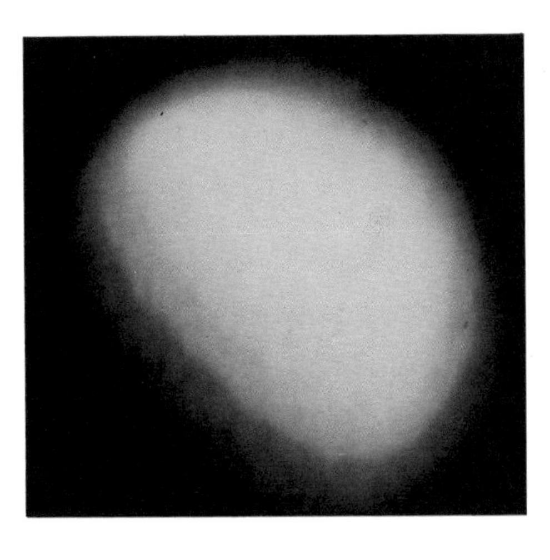

Rogue planets?

For a time it was thought that the New Zealand films might provide solid scientific evidence for UFOs.

Faced with this possibility, scientists were quick to react by putting forward a whole range of alternative explanations of what the object in the films might be. Some of their theories were wildly implausible – one even claimed the television crew had seen 'reflections from moonlight via cabbage leaves'. A more reasonable explanation was that the films showed a planet – but which one? One newspaper claimed it was Venus (left), another said it was Jupiter (right). But even the quickest glance at the planets themselves show these explanations to be unlikely. The *Daily Telegraph*, surprisingly, printed a strong condemnation of the Venus theory: 'The scientist who suggested that all [the television crew] were seeing was Venus on a particularly bright night can . . . be safely consigned to Bedlam.'

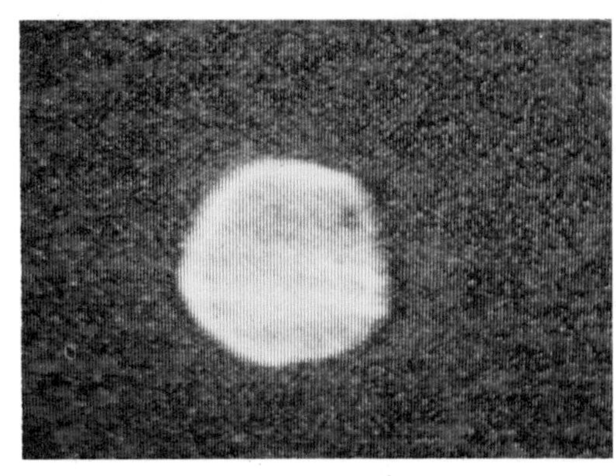

Right and far right: two stills from the New Zealand television crew's film. The presence of the strange objects was confirmed by Wellington air traffic control, who saw their traces on their radarscopes

Below: Captain Bill Startup, pilot of the aircraft from which the UFO film was taken

of the object with his hand-held camera. Dave Crockett has since explained that this changing of seats with the camera running was responsible for the violent shake seen at that point in the movie film.

After this, Bill Startup put the plane into another 360-degree turn. They then lost sight of the UFO, although Wellington control said its echo was still on the radar scope.

It should be noted that, although there was no room for a camera tripod to be mounted on the flight deck, the unidentified object stayed steady enough for David Crockett to be able to keep it dead centre in his camera viewfinder for more than 30 seconds.

As the plane approached Christchurch, the fuel gauge went into a spin, but the captain said that this occasionally happened and was not necessarily caused by interference by the UFO. At this point they were tuning in on the UFO off Banks Peninsula and were out of touch with Wellington control. Christchurch control had the object on its radar scope but later, when Captain Startup and American investigating scientist Dr Bruce Maccabee asked to see the radar tapes, the Christchurch supervisor replied that they had been 'wiped' clean as part of routine procedure.

The Argosy landed at Christchurch and journalist Dennis Grant joined the team in place of Dave Crockett's wife Ngaire. They left on the return flight to Blenheim at about 2.15 a.m. on 31 December 1978.

Early in this flight the observers saw two more strange objects. Through the camera lens Crockett saw what he described as a sphere with lateral lines around it. This object focused itself as Crockett watched through his camera – without adjusting the lens. He said the sphere was spinning. Significantly, one of the objects swayed on the Argosy's weather radar continuously for some 4 minutes. Later, as the aircraft approached Blenheim, they all saw two pulsating lights, one of which suddenly fell in a blurred streak for about 1000 feet (300 metres) before pulling up short in a series of jerky movements.

True or false?

Were the objects 'flying saucers'? Many alternative explanations were put forward: the film depicted a 'top secret American military remote-control drone vehicle', plasma or ball lightning, a hoax, meteorites, 'helicopters operating illegally at night', mutton birds, lights on Japanese squid boats, 'reflections from moonlight via cabbage leaves' (at Kaikoura), while Patrick Moore hedged his bets with a guess of 'a reflection, a balloon or an unscheduled aircraft.'

One newspaper claimed the film showed the planet Venus, out of focus because it was filmed with a hand-held camera. Another offered Jupiter as a candidate; an amateur astronomer had enhanced the light values of the film by putting through a line-scan analyser and had identified four small points of light that could be taken to correspond to the positions of the four largest moons of Jupiter. Venus and Jupiter appeared in different regions of the sky; because the television crew were so vague about the position of the lights relative to the aircraft as they were filming them, it was impossible to make a positive identification.

One of the most exciting aspects of the incident is that it appears to offer independent instrumental evidence of the sighting both on film and radar. But even here there are problems. Although both ground radar and the Argosy's own radar picked up unidentified traces, the number of UFOs the television crew claimed to have seen – about eight – conflicts with the 11 reported by ground radar. And the crew actually filmed only one object. The radar controller at Wellington, Ken Bigham, was dismissive about the whole affair:

> I managed to plot three of the echoes for 20 minutes or so before they faded completely. They definitely moved, varying between 50 and 100 knots (92.5 km/h and 185 km/h). I certainly couldn't identify them as anything. It's pretty inconclusive. They were purely the sort of radar echoes that constantly pop up. It is not unusual to get strange echoes appearing on what we call primary radar. They usually amount to nothing at all.

Nevertheless, the Royal New Zealand Air Force was concerned enough about the incident to put a Skyhawk jet fighter on full alert to intercept any other UFOs that might appear in the area. By the end of January, however, the fuss had died down and the New Zealand Defence Ministry stated that the radar images were 'spurious returns' and the unidentified objects 'atmospheric phenomena'.

What is the truth of the New Zealand affair? The film appears to be genuine; computer enhancement has not proved it to be a fake. It seems almost too good to be true that a television crew that had set out with the deliberate intention of filming 'flying saucers' should come up with such spectacular results; and yet it has to be assumed that the objects they saw were real enough to those who beheld them – and were not mere hallucinations. The case remains on file, a fascinating question mark.

Below: this unique frame from the New Zealand film seems to show the UFO performing an extraordinary feat of aerobatics – looping the loop in 1/24 of a second. An alternative explanation for this typical UFO behaviour: the hand-held camera was jogged

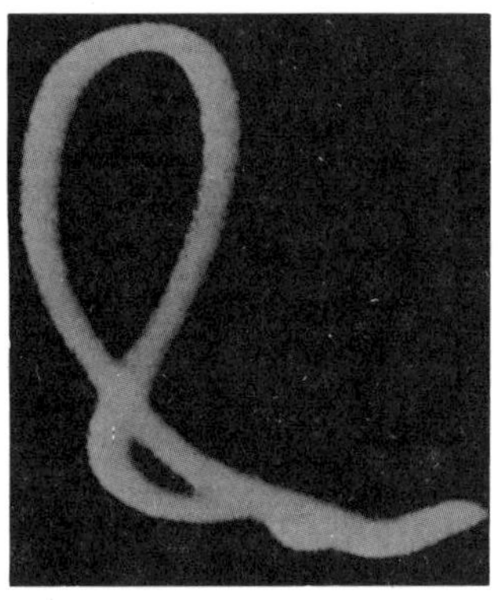

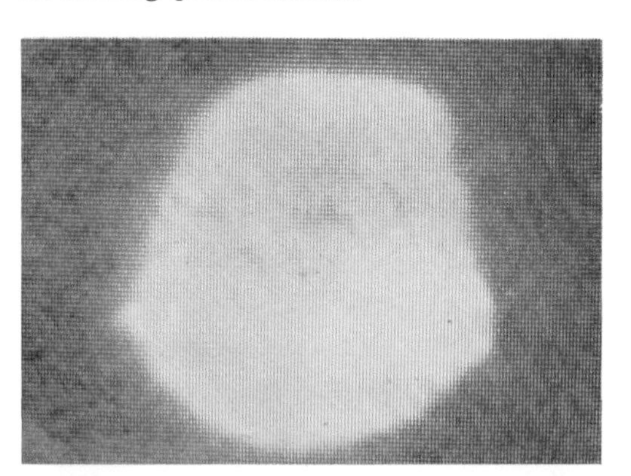

With the navigation lights of the aircraft switched off, the television crew was able to obtain this film of one of the objects. It pulsated from a pinpoint to the size of 'a large balloon'

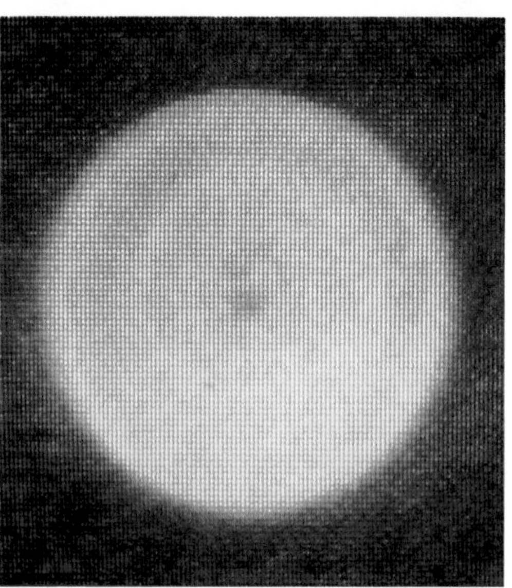

Silently, out of the night sky

SCIENTISTS GENERALLY consider UFOs that give responses on radar scopes the most reliable for their purposes. The first sighting described below took place at Caselle Airport in Turin, Italy, and is one of the most well-documented radar–visual sightings on record, while the second, at Ivinghoe, Bedfordshire, had only one witness, but its authenticity is vouched for by his sheer terror.

One of the most spectacular UFO waves lasted for five months in the winter of 1973 to 1974. It was heralded by the impressive sighting at Turin in November 1973—an event of profound significance for the science of ufology. It attracted the attention of Jean-Claude Bourret, a top reporter from the French radio station France-Inter, who broadcast a series of programmes about UFOs culminating in a startling and important interview with the then Minister of Defence, Monsieur Robert Galley.

The Ivinghoe incident, which took place 11 years earlier in 1962, shows a fascinating aspect common to many UFO reports—electromagnetic effects on electrical and mechanical equipment such as car radios.

'Sudden vast jumps to and fro'

Radar-visual: Caselle airport, Turin, Italy, 30 November 1973

On 30 November 1973 Riccardo Marano was preparing to land his Piper Navajo at Caselle Airport when he was advised by control that there was an unidentified object at a height of about 4000 feet (1200 metres) above the runway, close to where he was due to land. Control had the object on its radar screens and gave Marano permission to approach it to see what it was. As he neared his target, control reported that it was moving and was heading for the Suza Valley. Accordingly, Marano changed course to follow it – and suddenly control announced that the target had disappeared from its radar.

At that moment Marano received a message from another aircraft: the UFO was behind him at about 12,000 feet (3600 metres). Marano's Navajo was then flying at about 10,000 feet (3000 metres). He began to turn – and saw in front of him what appeared to be a bright white luminous sphere, which was emitting light of all colours of the spectrum. The light pulsated from bright to dim, but never went out completely. As he closed on the UFO, Marano reported that it was 'flying in a most irregular fashion, making fantastic lateral deviations and sudden vast jumps to and fro'. Taking advantage of a moment when the object was below him, Marano put his plane into a dive, accelerating to a speed of over 250 mph (400 km/h) – but he could not catch up with the UFO. When he gave up the chase, it was heading south-eastwards. He estimated its speed at about 550 mph (900 km/h).

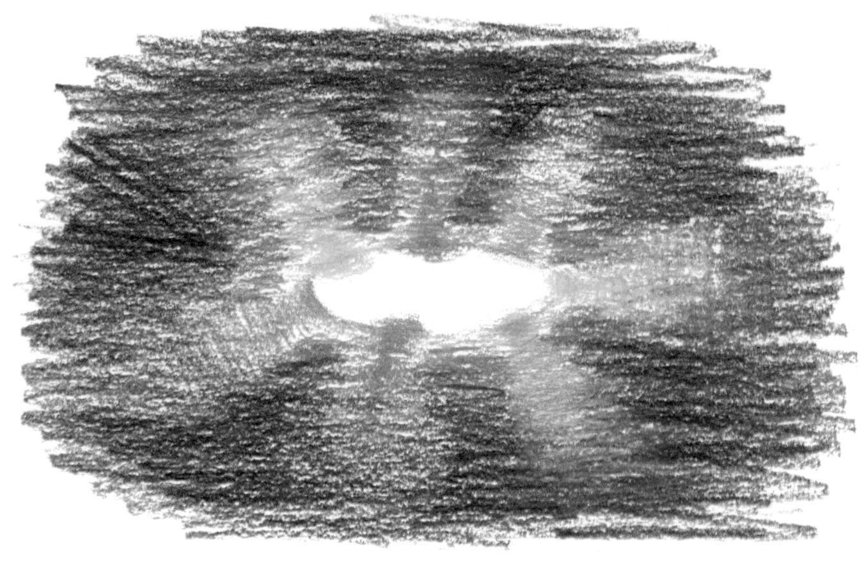

Two other pilots confirmed the presence of the object. They were Comandante Tranquillo, who had just taken off in his Alitalia DC-9, and Comandante Mezzalani, who was bringing his Alitalia DC-9 in from Paris. Comandante Tranquillo advised control that he dared not approach the 'shining object giving out flashes' and thereupon adjusted his course.

Comandante Mezzalani observed the object as he was touching down. He said it was large and bright, yet dimmer than a star or an artificial satellite.

There was another very reliable witness, none other than the commander of the neighbouring Caselle military airfield, Colonello Rustichelli, who stated that he had observed the UFO on his radar screen. It was, he said, something solid, which lit up like an aircraft on his radar, giving the same sort of return as would a DC-9. He said it looked like a star, but when he got it on his radar it stayed firm. Soon afterwards it headed off westwards.

A curious event, which may or may not be

connected with the UFO sightings described above, took place earlier on the same evening. At 5.00 p.m. Signor Franco Contin, an amateur photographer, saw an extremely bright object in the sky. At first he thought it was a star, but when he saw it begin to move about, he realised it must be something else. A slightly misshapen luminous globe, it was white at first and then suddenly turned deep orange. Signor Contin fetched his camera and took a total of eight photographs. These show an enormous object, oval in shape and brightly luminous.

The Turin sighting was remarkable not only because it was followed by a world-wide wave of UFO reports, but also because it attracted the attention of two very important people. The first of these was M. Jean-Claude Bourret of the French radio and television service ORTF, chief reporter of the radio station France-Inter, who was so impressed by the report of the sighting that he made a series of 39 radio programmes devoted to UFO research, which were broadcast between January 1973 and March 1974.

The other person whose interest was aroused by the Turin incident was Monsieur Robert Galley, Minister of Defence for France, who granted an exclusive interview to M. Bourret, which was broadcast on 21 February 1974.

Below: Monsieur Robert Galley in his historic interview with reporter Jean-Claude Bourret of the French radio station France-Inter on 21 February 1974. M. Galley admitted that the French government had been secretly studying UFOs for 20 years

This interview was of immense importance for the science of ufology – for in it a serving Minister of Defence admitted, not only that UFOs exist, but also that in 1954 his government had set up a secret section devoted to their study within the Ministry of Defence. M. Galley spoke of the massive nature of the UFO phenomenon, of the many detailed eyewitness reports he had read and of the volume of reports received from the Air Force in the early days of the project – in which, he said, 'the general agreement was quite disturbing'. Since 1970, UFO research in France has been in the hands of the *Centre National d'Etudes Spatiales* (The national centre for space studies), which evaluates reports of UFO sightings from both the Air Force and the Gendarmerie. Unfortunately, however, the French UFO group has no contact with international military groups.

M. Galley also admitted that 'it is certain that there are things that we do not understand and that are at present relatively inexplicable. I will indeed say that it is undeniable that there are things today that have not been explained or that have been incorrectly explained'.

This startling interview was immediately given wide coverage in the French papers, including *France-Soir, Le Parisien Libéré, L'Aurore* and *Le Figaro* and all the big provincial papers. It was soon reported in German, Spanish, Swiss, Italian, Brazilian and American newspapers – but not in the British press, or on radio or television. In his English translation of Jean-Claude Bourret's book *The crack in the universe* Gordon Creighton describes his unsuccessful attempts to convince the BBC that the interview was important enough to warrant a mention on one of its radio science programmes. He suggests that the scant and biased reporting of the UFO phenomenon by the British media may be the result of an official debunking attitude on the part of the authorities. Their methods are different from those used in the USA; indeed, says Mr Creighton,

> quieter and more subtle techniques of ridicule and denigration, plus, no doubt, the occasional discreet telephone call to the newspaper that has offended by printing a serious looking UFO report, have yielded far better results than the CIA's methods.

This scepticism on the part of the authorities no doubt accounts for the fact that very little serious scientific research is carried out into UFOs in Britain. Amateur UFO societies can do little more than monitor sightings. Suppression of information can only be harmful to research, and it is disturbing to think there may be many UFO sightings we simply never hear about.

'Like a halo round the moon'

Close encounter of the second kind: Ivinghoe, Bedfordshire, England, 9 February 1962

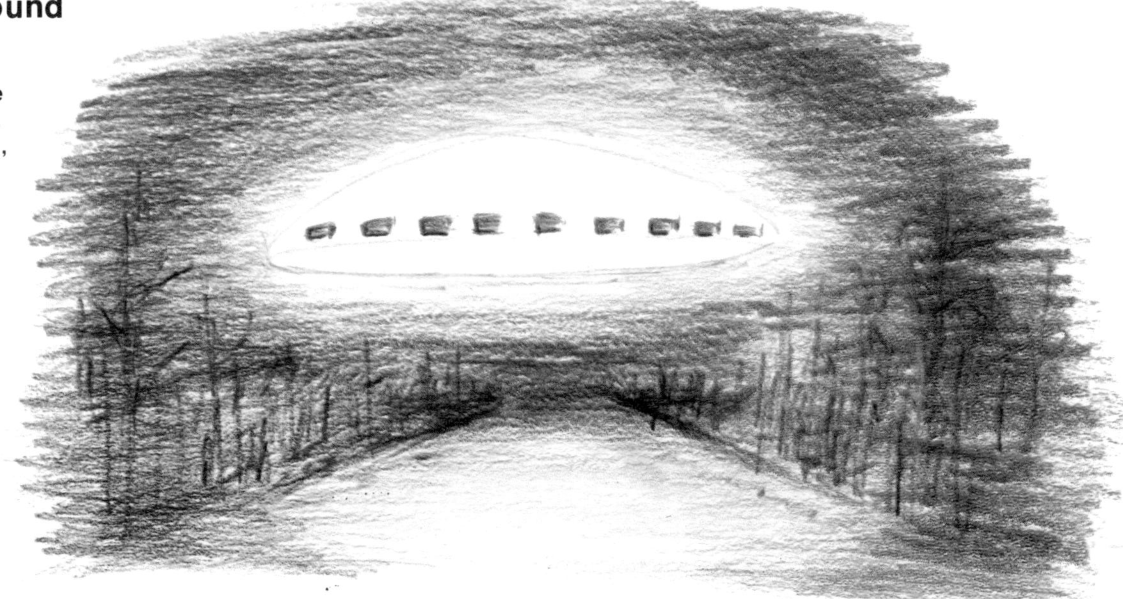

Mr Ronald Wildman, a delivery driver for the Vauxhall Motor Company, left his home in Luton, Bedfordshire, at 3.00 a.m. on 9 February 1962 to drive a new estate car from the factory to Swansea. He had passed Dunstable, and was on the Ivinghoe road approaching a set of crossroads at Tringford, when he saw an oval-shaped object ahead of him on the road. It was white with black markings at regular intervals around the perimeter. It appeared to be 20 to 30 feet (6 to 10 metres) above the road, and was at least 40 feet (12 metres) wide. Mr Wildman drove straight towards the object, but when he was 20 yards (18 metres) from it the power of the car's engine began to fade until he was going at just 20 mph (30 km/h). Putting his foot flat down on the accelerator did not help; neither did changing down through the gears. Mr Wildman noticed, however, that his headlights stayed on. For some 200 yards (180 metres) as he drove down the road, the UFO stayed about 20 feet (6 metres) ahead of, and above, him.

Suddenly a white haze appeared around the perimeter of the object – it was 'like a halo round the moon', said Mr Wildman – and it veered off to the right at high speed. As it went, it brushed particles of frost from the trees onto the windscreen of the Vauxhall.

In an interview, Mr Wildman recalled that his headlights were reflected from the object when it was closest to the road, and in his opinion this showed it was solid.

After the UFO had disappeared, the car's engine returned to normal working and the witness, by now panic-stricken, drove as hard as he could to Aylesbury where he reported the affair to the police. They noted the distraught condition of the driver.

The credibility of sightings with only one witness rests on the trustworthiness of the person concerned. Mr Wildman's report was checked by three investigators from *Flying Saucer Review*, who were extremely impressed by Mr Wildman's obvious sincerity. They were convinced his sighting had been genuine, not a hallucination.

Interference with electrical equipment such as televisions, car radios and headlights is a common feature of UFO reports. It has been suggested that this phenomenon may result from electromagnetic fields created by UFOs along their surfaces in order to minimise the effects of air resistance. Whatever the cause, this phenomenon can be one of the most frightening aspects of a UFO incident.

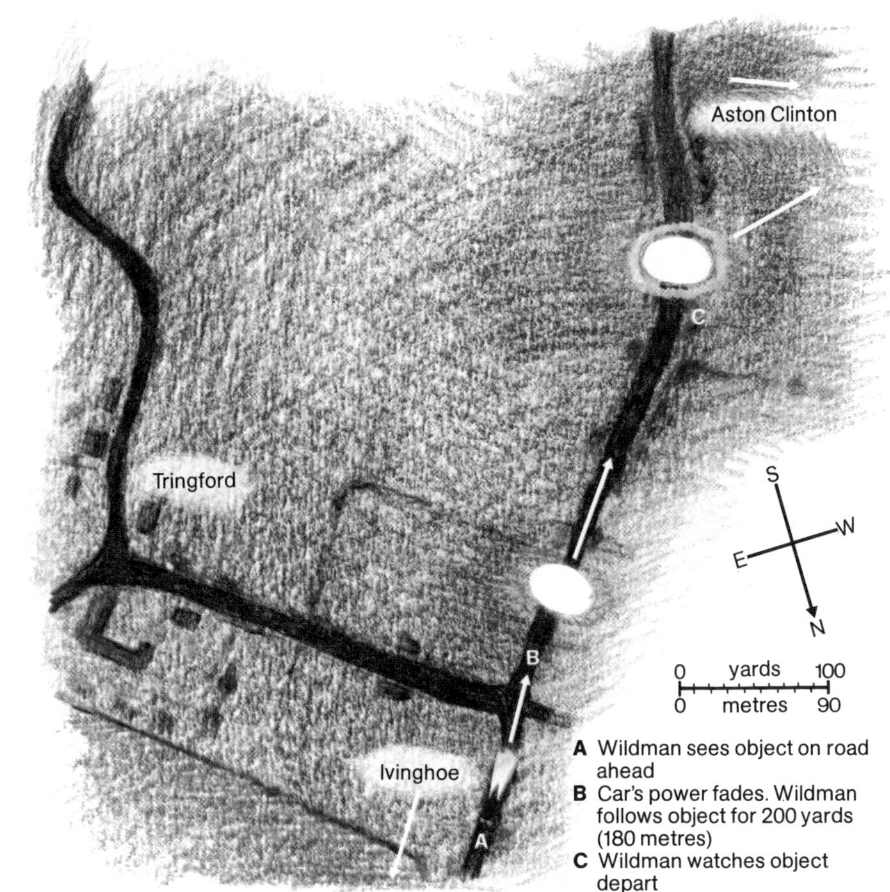

A Wildman sees object on road ahead
B Car's power fades. Wildman follows object for 200 yards (180 metres)
C Wildman watches object depart

Terror by night

DESPITE MANY people's scepticism about the existence and reported sightings of UFOs, some accounts are so vivid and detailed as to merit serious discussion. There are elements of the case of the Moreno family that inevitably keep alive the search for an explanation, in particular the length of time that members of the family were able to observe and what they had described they had seen invading their ranch.

'The figures were undoubtedly humanoid'

Close encounter of the third kind: Trancas, Argentina, 21 October 1963

At 7 p.m. on 21 October 1963 there was a breakdown of the private power plant of the Moreno family at their Santa Teresa Ranch, 2 miles (3 kilometres) from the small town of Trancas in the Tucumán province of Argentina. Since there was no light, the family retired to bed early, at about 8 p.m.; 21-year-old Señora Yolié de Valle Moreno (her maiden name is used at her request) stayed awake to feed her baby son.

Suddenly the maid, Dora Martina Guzman, 15, knocked on Yolié's door, crying that she was frightened. Yolié put this down to the loneliness of the place and took no notice. But moments later Dora Martina was back – there were strange lights outside the house, for which she could see no cause. She explained that every time she went outside the house the whole farmyard was suddenly lit up for a few seconds. This could not have been lightning; there was no thunderstorm brewing, and there were only a few clouds in the sky.

Yolié and her sister Yolanda got up and went outside the house to see for themselves. At first they could see nothing, but as they ventured further away from the house they saw, apparently on the railway line to the east, two bright, disc-shaped objects linked by a shining tube; Yolié described it as 'something like a small train, intensely illuminated'. A number of silhouettes – the sisters estimated about 40 – were moving about inside the tube. The figures were undoubtedly humanoid and the witnesses thought at first that there must have been a derailment on the line, or some sort of sabotage.

The sisters decided to go closer and investigate. They returned to the house for warm clothing, and Dora Martina fetched her Colt .38 pistol, which she kept as a safeguard for when she was alone in the house. Yolié woke her other sister Argentina, and asked her to listen for her baby. When Argentina heard what Yolié and Yolanda proposed to do she warned them of the dangers of guerillas and saboteurs and then, being curious, ventured outside to see for herself. She let out a terrified scream, shouting that there were strange machines near the house. As she ran away from them she fell over a pile of bricks that was lying in the yard.

Yolié, Yolanda and Dora Martina continued investigating; as they walked round the southern side of the house they could see a pale greenish light ahead of them near the front gate of the farm. They thought this must be from the headlights of the truck driven by one of the farm employees and Dora Martina ran forward to open the gate for it. As she ran ahead, Yolié shone her flashlight at the green light.

Instantly a disc-shaped, domed object was

revealed, hanging in mid-air in front of them. It had six brightly lit windows and was some 30 feet (9 metres) wide; metallic in appearance, it had a number of sections that were joined together with rivets at the seams. The dome was also metallic, but it was darker and had no rivets. The object was rocking gently to and fro.

Suddenly a multicoloured band began to rotate inside the windows and a whitish mist thickened around the object, which emitted a faint hum. The witnesses became aware of a sulphurous smell.

The three women took in all these details in less than 30 seconds. Then, without warning, a tongue of flame shot from the object, hit Dora Martina and hurled her and the two sisters to the ground. At the same time three more discs along the railway lit up, making six in all.

By now the parents, who had been woken by the sound of falling bricks, were watching the object nearest the house from the window of Argentina's room, which faced eastwards. As the band inside the craft rotated faster and faster, they watched while the disc gradually became enveloped in the white mist until all that could be seen was an orange-coloured cloud. A 'tube' of light emerged from the top of the object and probed the features of the house, as if conducting a careful scrutiny. Double 'tubes' of light probed forward from three of the objects on the railway line – one pair focused on a hen house, another on a tractor shed, and the third on a neighbour's house. The ends of these 'solid' light beams or tubes edged forwards slowly, penetrating a fence as they went.

It took a few minutes for the beams to cover the distance of 200 yards (180 metres) from the railway line to the shed, and they finally stopped about 6 feet (2 metres) from the front of the shed. The beams were perfectly cylindrical, about 10 feet (3 metres) wide. There were no shadows anywhere.

Recklessly, Yolié thrust her arm into one of the beams; she had been thinking that the beam might be a jet of water that had somehow been concentrated into a parallel-sided beam. What she felt, however, was a powerful sensation of heat – but there was no effect on her skin.

Yolié ran indoors. There, the temperature had risen from 60°F (16°C) to a stifling 104°F (40°C). The air was filled with a sulphurous smell and everyone felt burning, prickling sensations in their skin. Yolié's mother was praying, and Argentina and Yolanda were pleading with their father not to go outside.

The house was lit up as bright as day. Nobody was able to explain where the light was coming from; none of the witnesses noticed whether the light from the discs was passing through the walls of the house, though this is a possible 'explanation'.

The light had a powerful effect on the household animals. The Morenos owned three very fierce dogs and noticed that, whenever the light fell on the animals, they immediately became quiet and listless. When, occasionally, the beams fluctuated, the dogs seemed to come to life.

Next, the object closest to the house swung its tubular beam of light in the direction of Trancas. The beam advanced slowly for some 10 or 15 minutes until Yolié estimated it had reached the outskirts of Trancas; then, amazingly, it switched the tube in a U-turn back towards the house. Next it slowly withdrew the tube of light – which was, like the others, about 10 feet (3 metres) wide – until it vanished completely,

A Witnesses first see objects
B Large object becomes illuminated. Witnesses hurled to ground

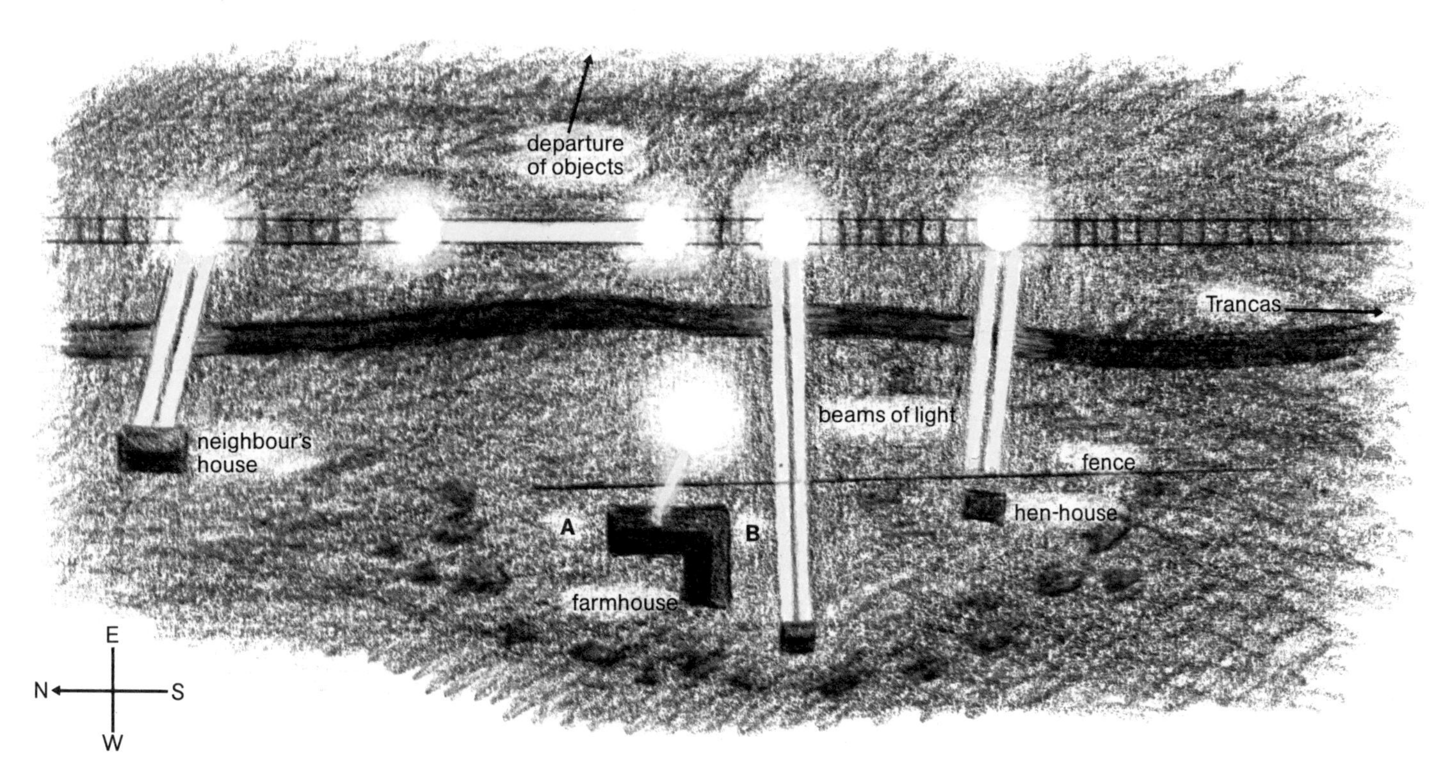

and then moved towards the other objects on the railway line. Finally all six objects rose and flew off at low altitude in an easterly direction towards a mountain range, the Sierra de Medina.

The time from the beginning of the sighting was then about 40 or 45 minutes. For more than half an hour after the objects had disappeared, the horizon was tinged with an orange glow. Once the Morenos had recovered from their shock, they ventured out into the garden. The cloud produced by the object that had been nearest to the house was still hanging in the air. It was very thick and there was a strong smell of sulphur. The cloud did not disperse until four hours later. A journalist who visited the family the next day said that the heat and the smell of sulphur inside the house were still quite striking.

Underneath the spot where the object had hovered the Morenos found, forming a perfect cone 3 feet (1 metre) high, a pile of small white balls half an inch (1 centimetre) in diameter. Next day they found similar little balls on the railway line.

The balls were found to disintegrate under gentle pressure. They were later analysed in the laboratories of the Institute of Chemical Engineering in the University of Tucumán and found to contain 96.48 per cent calcium carbonate and 3.51 per cent potassium carbonate.

An enquiry into the events at the Morenos' farmstead was quickly mounted by the local police. It was found that a Señor Jose Acosta and an entire family named Huanca had seen the strange illumination on the railway embankment, while a Señor Francisco Tropiano had seen the six discs flying across the sky at about 10.15 p.m., about the time the Morenos' ordeal had ended.

What was the purpose of this extraordinary siege of the lonely Argentinian ranch? It seems the alien pilots of the craft were conducting some kind of investigation – but what did they hope to find? Another possibility is that they were simply carrying out repairs to their craft. The light beams appear to have been used to discourage onlookers from approaching the craft. Whatever the purpose of the unknown pilots' visit, it seems they did not wish the Morenos any harm.

Aliens in the dark

THE UFO PHENOMENON often seems to veer into the realms of the psychic – indeed, some researchers believe UFOs to be from another dimension altogether. However, this view must be considerably modified when one comes across cases in which UFOs show up on radar screens, make deep marks in railway sleepers, or leave calcined stones behind as they did in these cases from England, France and Spain.

'Something is buzzing our airfield'

Radar-visual: Bentwaters, near Ipswich, England, 13 August 1956

THE NIGHT OF 13 August 1956 was a busy one for RAF and USAF air controllers and radar operators in East Anglia. Although some of the many inexplicable radar traces they obtained were probably spurious, others were undoubtedly from unknown objects. The sighting described here was stated by the USAF Condon Report as 'the most puzzling and unusual case in the radio-visual files'.

The main events began at 10.55 p.m. at RAF Bentwaters, near Ipswich, a station leased to the United States Air Force. A Ground Controlled Approach (GCA) radar operator picked up a fast-moving target 30 miles (50 kilometres) to the east, heading in from the sea at a speed of 2000 to 4000 miles per hour (3200 to 6440 km/h). It passed directly over Bentwaters and sped away until it disappeared from the scope 30 miles (50 kilometres) to the west. This overflight was not just a radar observation, however; a tower operator on the ground looking up saw a light 'blurred out by its high speed', while the pilot of a USAF C-47 aircraft flying over Bentwaters at 4000 feet (1200 metres), who had been alerted by ground control, looked down and saw the fuzzy light flash between his aircraft and the ground. The UFO was heading towards Lakenheath, another RAF aerodrome leased to the USAF, and immediate warning was given.

For the record, there was no mention of a sonic boom at Bentwaters. Ground observers at Lakenheath saw the light approach, stop dead, and then move swiftly out of sight to the east. Some time after that two white lights were seen; they joined up and disappeared in formation.

Observers and radar operators of the Lakenheath GCA and radar traffic control centre scopes testified to having recorded objects travelling at terrific speeds, stopping, and changing course instantaneously. After some hesitation the Americans at Lakenheath put through a call to the RAF.

The RAF Chief Controller at Bentwaters remembers USAF at Lakenheath telephoning to say something was 'buzzing' their airfield circuit. He scrambled a Venom night fighter from RAF Waterbeach, and his interception controller, with a team of three highly

trained personnel, took over. The Venom was vectored onto the UFO and the pilot, who was accompanied by a navigator, called out 'Contact' when he could see it, and 'Judy' when the navigator had the target fairly and squarely on the fighter's own radar scope. The Venom closed on the target but after a few seconds, and in the space of one or two sweeps on the scopes, the object appeared behind the fighter. The pilot called out 'Lost contact, more help,' and he was told that the target was now behind him.

Meanwhile the chief controller scrambled another Venom fighter. The American witnesses said the UFO 'flipped over' and got behind the RAF fighter, which then manoeuvred to try to get behind the UFO. This information was given to the USAF-sponsored study of the UFO phenomenon under Dr E. U. Condon at Colorado University. Until the Condon Report was published in January 1969 the case had remained secret. A detailed study was carried out by Dr James McDonald, an upper atmosphere physicist at Arizona University. This was a sighting the Condon Report could not dismiss; indeed, it had to admit that 'the apparently rational, intelligent behavior of the UFO suggests a mechanical device of unknown origin as the most probable explanation.'

'Two very odd creatures'

Close encounter of the third kind: Quarouble, near Valenciennes, France, 10 September 1954

The small French village of Quarouble, not far from Valenciennes close to the Belgian border, was shaken by the events of the night of 10 September 1954.

At about 10.30 p.m., 34-year-old Monsieur Marius Dewilde was sitting reading in the kitchen of his little house. His wife and son were already in bed. The house was situated among woods and fields just under a mile from the village. There was a fenced garden in front of the house, and to one side of this there ran a National Coal Mines railway track between St Amand-les-Eaux and the giant Blanc Misseron steel works where M. Dewilde was employed.

Suddenly his dog started to bark and howl and, thinking there was a prowler or smuggler outside the house, M. Dewilde took his flashlight and ventured out into the darkness. He was instantly aware of an ill-defined shape to his left, on or near the railway line; he thought it might be a farmer's truck. Then, as his dog came up to him, cringing on her belly, he heard a sound to his right. He swung round, and his torch beam fell on two very odd creatures, each just over 3 feet (1 metre) tall and wearing what appeared to be a diver's suit. M. Dewilde said they seemed to be shuffling along on very short legs. He noticed that they had very broad shoulders, but no arms and that they wore huge helmets. They were heading for the dark shape he had seen on the railway line.

Recovering from his initial surprise, the tough, taciturn steel worker ran to the garden gate with the intention of cutting off the interlopers from the path. He was about 2 yards (2 metres) from them when a blinding beam of light, the colour of magnesium flares, issued from an opening in the side of the dark shape. The beam struck him and he was stopped dead in his tracks, unable to move or shout; it was as though he were paralysed, he said. With a sense of horror he watched the two creatures pass within a yard (1 metre) of him, and on towards the still indistinguishable shape.

Suddenly the light went out and, recovering the use of his muscles, M. Dewilde set off after the small creatures. All he saw, however, was what appeared to be a door closing in the side of the object, which then rose slowly from the ground like a helicopter. There was a whistling noise, and M. Dewilde saw steam clouding up from beneath the contraption. After rising about 30 yards (30 metres) the craft – if that is what it was – set off towards the east, climbing and glowing red as it went.

Shocked, and in a highly agitated state, M. Dewilde woke up his wife, then ran off to the police station in the village. The policemen on duty thought he was out of his mind and sent him on his way. But he contrived to get access to the Commissioner who, after listening to his semi-coherent account, realised that this man – by now in a state of incontinence – was neither joking nor mad.

A detailed enquiry was set up by the regular police, the air gendarmerie and the

Territorial Security Department. They were convinced that the witness was not lying. They were convinced, too, that the object could not have been a helicopter (carrying contraband for example) because of the mass of telephone wires overhead which would have prevented a landing.

It was suggested by one journalist that M. Dewilde was suffering from the effects of a head wound, and had had an hallucination, but this theory was untenable in view of the discovery of marks, sharply and deeply cut, in the iron-hard wood of the railway sleepers where M. Dewilde said the object had stood. A railway engineer calculated that it would have taken a weight of 30 tons (30 tonnes) to have made the marks. It would have taken great heat to have produced the burnt and calcined ballast stones found between the affected sleepers, and this would have called for an extremely powerful hallucination!

'As big as a jumbo-jet'

Radar-visual: Valencia, Spain, 11 November 1979

On Sunday evening, 11 November 1979, a Supercaravelle of the Spanish airline TAE, on a charter flight from Salzburg to Tenerife, put down unexpectedly at Valencia in Spain. The flight had been four hours late in starting, and this extra delay was almost the last straw for the tourists on board the aeroplane. Fortunately, most of them were unaware of what had gone on outside – 24,000 feet (7000 metres) above the Mediterranean.

The incident began after the aeroplane had passed over Ibiza. In an interview with newsman Juan J. Benítez, the skipper, Commandante Lerdo de Tejada, said that a few minutes before 11 p.m. he was requested by Air Control in Barcelona to tune in to radio frequency 121.5 megahertz, an emergency wavelength. He picked up the hiss of the carrier wave but received no instructions. Before the captain could query this he saw two powerful red lights at the 'nine o'clock' position (to the left, or port side).

Commandante Tejada thought there was only one 'thing' carrying two lights. This object bore down on them at great speed, coming up on their left, and a little behind them. He added:

> When we saw them first they were at about 10 miles [16 kilometres]. Then they made towards us and literally 'played' with us at about half-a-mile [1 kilometre] . . . the object was moving upwards and downwards at will, all around us, and performing movements that would be quite impossible for any conventional machine to execute.

According to the captain the object seemed to be as big as a jumbo-jet. Finally, he said, the speed and closeness of this monstrous object were such that he was forced to perform a 'break' – a sharp turn to avoid possible collision – about 60 miles (100 kilometres) from Valencia. Air Control in Barcelona were informed that unidentified traffic was close by, and that the UFO had stayed near to the aircraft for eight minutes. After the 'break' the UFO followed the jet for another 30 miles (50 kilometres).

The controls and instruments of the Supercaravelle were not affected during the emergency. The automatic pilot did, in fact, fail – but that, said the captain, was not due to the UFO. Finally Manises Airport at Valencia was contacted and permission was requested to make an emergency landing, The Supercaravelle touched down a few minutes before midnight.

Señor Morlan, director of the airport, his traffic controller and other personnel confirmed seeing an extraordinary object with red lights over the airport.

Señor Benítez also found that there had been a vigorous response to the alert by the Spanish Air Force as military radars had picked up unidentified targets in the precise area where the TAE airliner was flying. The unidentified echoes persisted and two F-1 fighters were scrambled from Los Llanos five minutes after the Supercaravelle had landed. It is understood that visual contact was made – and that one of the fighters was subjected to a number of close approaches by the UFO.

UFO Photo File

Above: this photograph was taken by a coastguard, R. Alpert, at 9.35 a.m. on 16 July 1952 from the control tower at Salem Air Base in Massachusetts, USA. The objects were reported to be moving at great speed. They appear much brighter in the photograph than they actually were because the aperture of the camera was set for the brightness of the surrounding landscape and consequently the UFOs themselves are overexposed.

But is the photograph genuine? The images are unlikely to have been caused by lens flares, as these almost always appear in straight lines. But it is reported that the picture was taken through a laboratory window – and sceptics have suggested that the objects could actually be reflections of lights inside the laboratory. Photographic experts, however, point out that reflected lights are rarely as opaque as these.

Right: this picture, published here for the first time, was taken by London photographer Anwar Hussein in the Spanish Pyrenees in July 1978. After finishing filming one day, he found he had left one of his lenses at the top of a mountain. The next morning, about 9 o'clock, he returned to look for it. Mr Hussein found the lens and took some pictures; his camera was set on motor-drive. At the time he noticed nothing unusual – except the brightness of the light and the uncanny quietness. Back in London, he sent the film to be developed – and received a worried telephone call from the lab, who pointed out the 'object' on the film and thought it must be a fault that had appeared during developing. On examination, however, the emulsion was found to be undamaged. This is typical of many of the best UFO pictures, which are often of objects that go unnoticed at the time of filming.

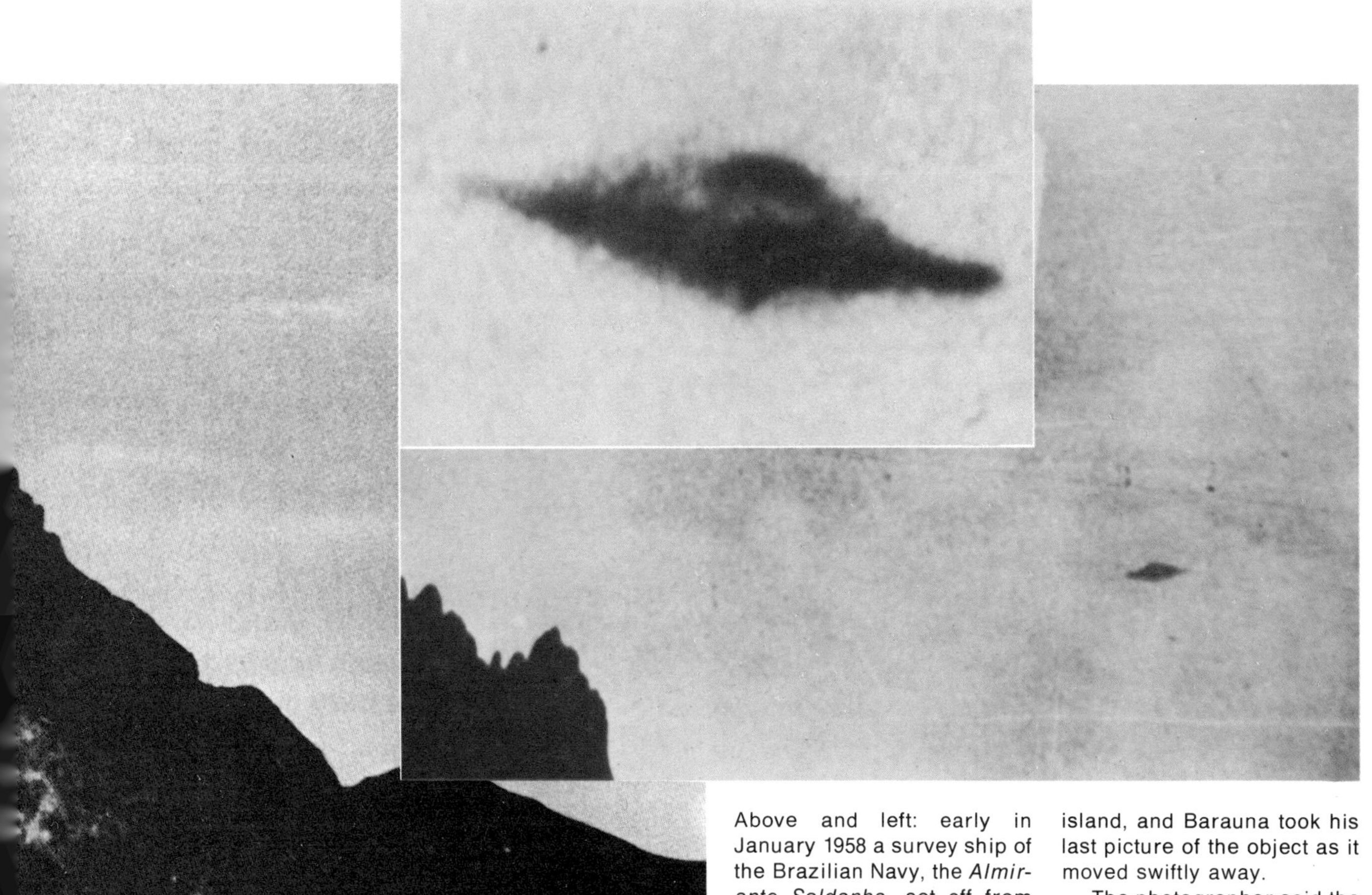

Above and left: early in January 1958 a survey ship of the Brazilian Navy, the *Almirante Saldanha*, set off from Rio de Janeiro bound for the rocky island of Trindade, where the Navy had an oceanographic station. Among those on board was Almiro Barauna, a specialist in underwater photography.

Just before the ship was due to set sail on the return journey at 12.15 p.m. on 16 January 1958, a retired Air Force officer, Captain Viegas, who was on deck with other officers and technicians, called to Barauna that there was a bright object in the sky. Barauna located it and watched the moving object until it was silhouetted against some cloud. Then he shot two photographs. The UFO then disappeared behind the main peak of the island for a few seconds. When it reappeared it was flying in the opposite direction. Barauna took a third photograph, then a fourth and fifth, but these last two were wasted shots because the photographer was jostled by the other people aboard the ship, who were by now extremely excited. The UFO appeared briefly to halt its passage away from the island, and Barauna took his last picture of the object as it moved swiftly away.

The photographer said the object was silent, dark grey in colour, and was apparently surrounded by a greenish vapour or mist.

Barauna developed his film on board ship in the presence of the skipper, Commander Bacellar. (As there was no photographic paper on board, prints were made when the ship had returned to Rio.) Barauna said that in the urgency and excitement of the sighting, he did not think to check the settings of his camera and the pictures were consequently over-exposed.

Back in Rio de Janeiro, the Brazilian Navy examined the negatives. They found them to be genuine, and any possibility of a hoax was eliminated. Based on Barauna's account, the naval authorities set up a mock re-run of the incident, and were able to compute the speed of the object as about 550 to 600 mph (900 to 1000 km/h). The diameter of the Saturn-shaped UFO was estimated at around 40 yards (37 metres). At least 100 people had seen the UFO – and the photographs seem to be unimpeachable.

Grand UFO spectaculars

ONE RECURRENT FEATURE of UFO reports is the seeming pointlessness of the incidents – lights that hover in the skies, 'buzz' aircraft or frighten small groups of witnesses, all to no apparent purpose. Here we describe two extraordinary UFO events. The first is from the Canary Islands, where a UFO appeared before large numbers of people at a distance, as well as treating three terrified witnesses to a close-up display involving the humanoid 'pilots' of the craft. The second story comes from Lot-et-Garonne in south-west France, where a UFO appeared silently above a field in which a farmer was working one night, frightening him half out of his wits – and then simply, and silently, disappeared.

'Two enormous beings'

Close encounter of the third kind: Canary Islands, Spain, 22 June 1976

On the evening of 22 June 1976 an extremely active UFO visited the Canary Islands. It was witnessed by many people, and a number of reports found their way into the Spanish press. There the matter would, no doubt, have rested but – in a surprise turn of events – the Spanish Air Ministry released documentation on 12 UFO incidents to journalist Juan José Benítez of the Bilbao newspaper *La Gaceta del Norte*. One of the cases listed in their dossier was the extraordinary Canary Islands spectacular.

Some interesting facts emerged. A report by a doctor on the island of Gran Canaria had already achieved international publicity, and apparently the events had been confirmed by a Spanish warship and by photographs taken by a private citizen (later impounded to be examined by the authorities).

At 9.27 p.m. on 22 June 1976 the Captain, an ensign and several crewmen of the Spanish Navy corvette *Atrevida* spotted the UFO off the south-eastern coast of the island of Fuerteventura. They saw a light, part yellowish and part blue, moving across the sea towards them, gaining altitude. They thought at first that they were watching an aeroplane with its landing lights on, but then rapidly revised that opinion when the light stopped suddenly and was abruptly extinguished, only to be replaced by a rotating beam of light shining downwards. Two minutes later the light took the form of a great halo that lasted for some 40 minutes, lighting up both land and sea. The original yellow-bluish light now reappeared, splitting into two parts, the bluish part remaining within the halo while the upper part began to climb in an irregular spiral before vanishing in the direction of the neighbouring island of Gran Canaria. It took only three minutes to get there, reaching the astonishing speed, over 85 nautical miles (158 kilometres), of some 1900 miles per hour (3060 km/h).

There were a number of witnesses to the UFO in the northern part of Gran Canaria but the one with the best story to tell was the local doctor, Don Francisco-Julio Padrón León. He had been called out by a young man, Santiago del Pino, to attend his sick mother. The doctor and the young man were travelling in a taxi driven by Francisco Estévez, which had just negotiated a bend in the road at a place called Las Rosas (between Gàldar and

Below: an impressive photograph of the Canary Islands UFO taken by a private citizen. This was impounded for examination by the Spanish police and not released until some months after the incident

Agaete in the north-western corner of the island). Suddenly they found themselves confronted by a giant sphere hanging a few yards from the ground. The sphere was outlined in a pale greyish-blue. Almost instantly the radio in the taxi cut out and the three witnesses shivered as they felt a surging wave of cold.

The taxi driver had stopped his vehicle. He was trembling with cold as all three men watched two enormous beings apparently inside the sphere (which was the size of a two-storey house and quite transparent – the stars behind it could be seen quite clearly). There were panels of instruments on a kind of platform inside the sphere.

The two ufonauts seemed to be clad in tight-fitting clothing in a deep shade of red and wore black helmets. No features were described in the witnesses' statements, but the creatures were seen in profile. They stood facing one another on either side of an instrument console, manipulating levers and switches with hands that were enclosed in black cones. Dr Padrón was particularly impressed by the disproportionate size of the backs of their heads.

Suddenly the taxi driver took it into his head to switch on the spotlight. At that instant the sphere began to rise until the watchers could see a transparent tube inside it that emitted a blue gas or liquid. This gradually filled the sphere, which expanded until it was as big as a 30-storey building although the beings and their console panels remained the same size.

Greatly alarmed, the driver turned the car and back-tracked to some nearby houses where a family who lived in one of them told the doctor that their television had blacked out. The witnesses joined the family in the house and, as they watched the extraordinary object from the windows, they saw the blue 'gas' stop swirling inside the sphere. Then the object emitted a high-pitched whistle and flashed away in the direction of Tenerife, changing as it went to a 'spindle' shape surrounded by a halo.

It is now known that Dr Padrón was instructed by the Spanish Air Ministry investigators not to speak about his experience. Consequently details of his statements were not known until the dossier was handed over

to Senor Benítez. However, a sketchy outline of the story had leaked out before the restriction was applied. Some newspapers carried the story about a large spherical object that had been seen with control panels and 'pilots' visible inside, hovering over an onion field where part of the crop was destroyed. The destruction of a circular area about 33 yards (30 metres) in diameter was confirmed in the Ministry file.

The UFO was next seen by hundreds of people in Puerto de la Cruz as it passed over the island of Tenerife, then by the crew and passengers of a ferry plying between Tenerife and La Palma – while many inhabitants of the outlying islands of Gomera and Hierro telephoned newspaper offices and local radio stations about their sightings of the object.

The Ministry's dossier contained a report that the object had been detected and followed on radar along with prints from photographs of the UFO taken from the southern part of Gran Canaria. The photographer had been located by the police and his film had been impounded until the release of the dossier some months later.

The doctor's testimony gives the impression that he witnessed a truly unique UFO 'display'. But as ever, the question remains: was it an exhibition of remote control?

Over the years there has been a great deal of speculation about the nature of the objects seen by UFO witnesses. Are UFOs, in fact, some kind of projection from the controllers of the phenomenon? And if so, who – or what – are these controllers, and why will they not show themselves to us? What is the message they are trying to give us?

'All around . . . was bathed in light'

Close encounter of the first kind: Lot-et-Garonne, France, 13–14 November 1971

The weather in Lot-et-Garonne in southwestern France, 56 miles (90 kilometres) east of the city of Bordeaux, on the night of Saturday, 13 November 1971, was miserable. The sky was overcast and there was a drizzling rain. Nevertheless farmer Angelo Cellot was out working, ploughing a field that adjoined the minor road between his house and that of his brothers. Monsieur Cellot's tractor was fitted with headlights and a movable spotlight – for he was accustomed to working late into the night.

At about 1.50 a.m. he suddenly became aware of a light that he first thought was from another farmer's tractor. However, as he turned his tractor at the road's edge and proceeded in the opposite direction towards the stream at the northern boundary, he realised the light was in the air, and moving along the stream towards his field. He thought it was a helicopter, but as he turned again towards the road he realised the object had changed direction and was following him up the field, preceded by a red light. The UFO, hovering at an estimated altitude of 130 feet (40 metres), had five bright lights underneath it, so bright that when he trained the spotlight onto it Angelo could not distinguish any shape behind them.

The farmer had reached the end of the furrow close to the road when he realised the aerial intruder was directly overhead. All around him was bathed in light from the five beams, and now puzzled concern gave way to fear. He saw that the UFO was descending and was already only 50 to 70 feet (15 to 20 metres) above him. Fear changed to panic. Angelo deserted his tractor, leaving the engine running and headlights on, and dashed away towards his brother Jean's house to raise the alarm. He had covered about 30 yards (30 metres) when he looked back and saw the UFO climbing and heading away to the north. So he ran back, and switched off lights and engine. It was only then that he realised the object had been completely silent. As Angelo watched he saw, to his relief, the UFO slowly disappear from sight beyond a low ridge.

Thoroughly shaken, and with no wish to finish his job, the farmer put the tractor in its barn and went to bed at 2 a.m.

This important story eventually reached the newspaper *La Dépêche du Midi*, and thence the French investigatory group GEPA, for whom Colonel Pierre Berton interviewed Angelo Cellot. He was accompanied at the interview by two officers of the Gendarmerie, and later made an official report.

As in many other reports the predominant feature of this UFO sighting is *light*; glowing light, opalescent light, haloes of light, coloured light, revolving light, beams of light, and the mysterious *solid* beams of light. But here the similarity ends; the 'light shows' display a bewildering variety. How should we make sense of it?

The Rex Heflin photographs

UFO sightings are generally worth taking seriously if they satisfy two criteria: they are made by reliable witnesses and supported by some form of independent evidence. Yet here is a report that presents the serious investigator with an unsatisfactory number of loose ends – even though it was made by a responsible highway official and comes armed with what are, if they are authentic, some of the best UFO pictures ever taken.

'Too controversial'

Daylight disc: Santa Ana, California, USA, 3 August 1965

Right: photograph 1 (see map overleaf), taken by Rex Heflin of the UFO he saw near Santa Ana, California, USA. The photographs were taken with a Polaroid camera through the windscreen of the truck in which Heflin was sitting at the time of the sighting

One of the most impressive sets of photographs of an alleged UFO is that taken by Mr Rex Heflin at 12.38 p.m. (Daylight Saving Time) on 3 August 1965, on the Myford Road near the Santa Ana Freeway outside Los Angeles in California, USA. Heflin, who had been a police officer for four years, was working for the Orange County Highways Department at the time when he took the photographs.

In his report of the sighting, Heflin stated that, at about 11.30 on the morning of 3 August, his truck was standing facing north-north-east at the side of Myford Road, within sight of the junction of the Santa Ana Freeway. He was attempting to make contact on his two-way radio with the road maintenance superintendent, to report that tree limbs were obscuring the view of a railroad crossing sign, when the radio went dead.

All at once he caught sight of what he thought, at first, was an aircraft, approaching from the left (north-north-west) – but, seconds later, he realised it was a disc with a domed top.

He reached for his Polaroid Model 101 camera, which was standard equipment for Orange County Road Department officials, and took his first photograph, through the windscreen of his truck.

Heflin claimed that the object moved slowly in an arc over the road, and to the right of his truck. He took his second picture, again through the windscreen. He took the third picture just before the UFO, which had

Right: photograph 2. The object had now moved across Myford Road, and changed direction abruptly before photograph 3 was taken

suddenly 'wobbled' once or twice, gained altitude and accelerated in a wide arc beyond the Freeway towards the north-west. When asked whether the bottom of the UFO appeared to have any markings, openings or evidence of landing gear, Heflin replied:

> No! The only thing I saw on the bottom of the craft was a white beam of light emitting from the centre and sweeping in a circle to the outer edge of the craft. The movement of the beam was similar to the sweep of a radar scope beam.

Suddenly the craft was gone, leaving a ring of smoke, or vapour, in the air. Heflin said he drove up the road and stopped near the ring, jumped from his cab, and photographed the ring before it disappeared.

The witness returned to his truck and found that his radio was working again. The same afternoon, after duty, he returned to the office and showed his colleagues his UFO photographs. During the first few days after the sighting, comments the Condon report, Heflin allowed many of his friends to make copies of his pictures; 'time passed and apparently more copies of the pictures were made and handed out to various friends of friends, until most of Santa Ana was saturated with the UFO pictures.'

One of Heflin's friends, having first obtained his permission, sent copies of the photographs to *Life* magazine. According to the Condon commission report they were rejected as being 'too controversial' – even though they were 'the best that *Life* had seen so far.'

News of Heflin's sighting came to the attention of the local newspaper, the *Santa Ana Register*, which tracked Heflin down and invited him to show them the photographs. These created great interest, and enlargements were made – and 'cropped' – for printing; the first picture appeared in an article in the *Santa Ana Register* on 20 September 1965.

Needless to say, Rex Heflin came under a great deal of pressure to supply copies of his photographs to interested groups and investigators, but curiously enough he was unable to supply any *original* prints. He claimed that the negatives from which the *Register* had made its prints were made from the original Polaroid prints, and that he himself had been present while the film was being processed – but the newspaper insisted that its prints were from Polaroid *copies*.

From this point a whole new mystery blew up around the affair, for Heflin claimed that he had handed over the original prints to a man with impressive credentials who had claimed to come from North American Air Defense (NORAD). Unfortunately Heflin did not ask for a receipt for his photographs, and he claims they were never returned to him. Months later NORAD denied having had anything to do with the incident and, according to the *Orlando Sentinel*, a Florida newspaper, among others, Colonel George P. Freeman, the Pentagon spokesman for Project Blue Book, stated that similar 'mystery men' in a number of States, claiming to represent NORAD and various other government agencies, were confronting and 'silencing' witnesses of UFOs.

A general air of confusion and speculation surrounded the Heflin photographs. Then, in April 1969, new light was thrown on the subject when aerospace engineer John R. Gray, who had formerly worked on the Apollo space programme, published a study in *Flying Saucer Review* that gave considerable support to Rex Heflin's claims.

Working from an uncropped enlargement of the first photograph – which showed, on the road, the shadow of the telegraph (utility) pole 26 feet (8 metres) from the camera

Below: photograph 3. Heflin took this picture just before the UFO, which had wobbled once or twice, gained altitude and moved beyond the Santa Ana Freeway (marked by telegraph wires in the photograph) to the north-west

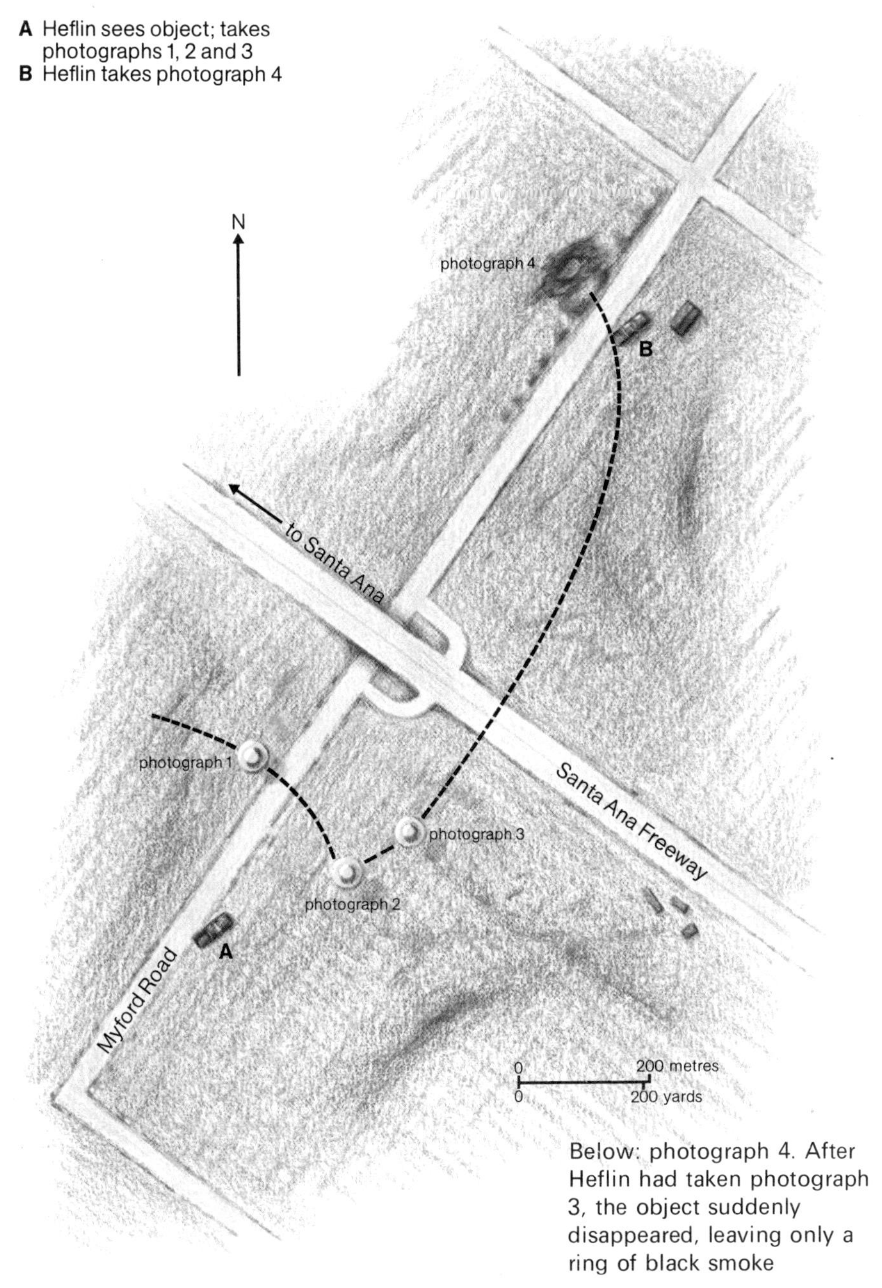

Below: photograph 4. After Heflin had taken photograph 3, the object suddenly disappeared, leaving only a ring of black smoke

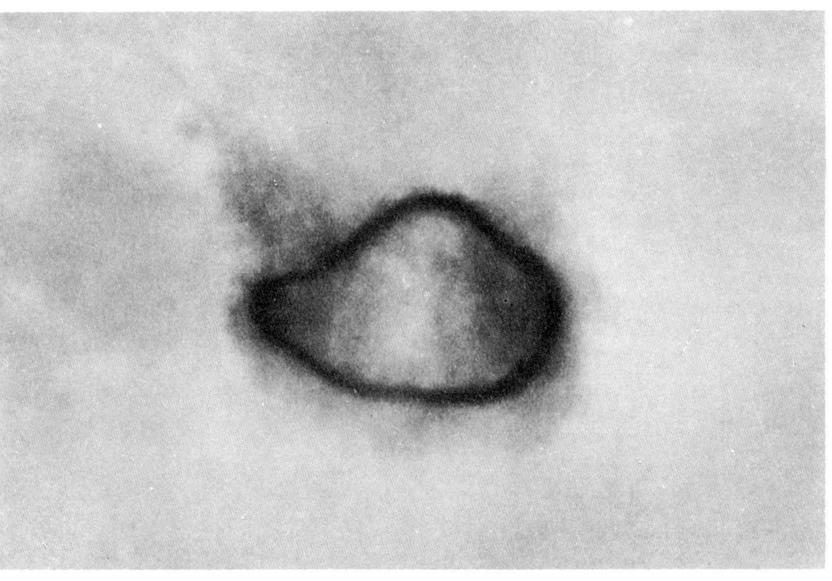

position – he calculated the elevation and the azimuth of the sun at the time of the sighting to be 72°46′ and 162°51′ respectively. Using these figures, he was able to establish that the true time of the sighting was 12.38 p.m., Daylight Saving Time; Heflin, who had no watch, had estimated the time at 11.30 a.m. Mr Gray also pointed out that, because the alleged UFO cast no shadow on the road, its diameter could not lie within the range of $10\frac{1}{2}$ inches (27 centimetres) to 6 feet (1.8 metres).

This statement was based upon calculations of possible altitude and distance of the object from the camera. For instance, if the diameter of the object were 6 feet (1.8 metres), the distance from the camera would have been 143.1 feet (43.6 metres). For comparison, the vertical, white irrigation pipe that can be seen on the left-hand side of the road in the photograph was 245 feet (75 metres) from the camera position.

Mr Gray worked out that, if the object had been 6 feet (1.8 metres) wide, its altitude would have been 28.7 feet (8.7 metres). At this altitude, the object would have cast a shadow on the road that would have been visible in the photograph. Heflin himself had estimated the diameter of the object to be 30 feet (9 metres); if this were so, Mr Gray estimated the horizontal distance of the camera from the alleged UFO to be 723 feet (220 metres) and its altitude to be 134.5 feet (40 metres). These figures were fairly close to Heflin's estimates; he thought the object was half a mile (800 metres) away, flying at an altitude of about 150 feet (45 metres).

While many people believe the Heflin photographs to be genuine pictures of a UFO, others have suggested that the whole affair is probably a hoax. The story has a number of curious features and some small inconsistencies. And it is unfortunate, and some people think suspicious, that the original photographs have not survived.

The American UFO organisation Ground Saucer Watch has subjected Rex Heflin's photographs to rigorous computer analyses – and has concluded that they are probably fakes. However it is only fair to mention that GSW has been wrong in the past.

The incident was investigated by Dr W. Hartmann of the Condon Commission. He concluded that the case was of 'little probative value': the photographs contained 'no geometric or physical data that permit a determination of distance or size independent of the witness's testimony.' Dr Hartmann also commented that he had been able to simulate the first three photographs by 'suspending a model by a thread attached to a rod resting on the roof of a truck and photographing it.' Although, as he says himself, this does not *prove* the Heflin pictures are fakes, it certainly detracts from their value as evidence for the existence of UFOs.

Radar echoes and angel hair

In 1957 an unidentified object accompanied a US Air Force aircraft for over 800 miles (1300 kilometres) on a military manoeuvre, and was traced all the way on radar. Was it scrutinising the aircraft? Or was it simply making its presence known? Three years earlier a rural district of south-western France was treated to two identical UFO displays. These spectaculars, though apparently pointless, seemed nevertheless to be trying to convey some kind of message. But were they? And if so, what was it?

'Bigger than a house'

Radar-visual: south-eastern United States, 19 September 1957

Right: an RB-47 photo-reconnaissance aircraft

Below: how directions are given in the air. The aircraft lies at the centre of an imaginary clock, so an object 90° to the right of the aircraft is 'at 3 o'clock'

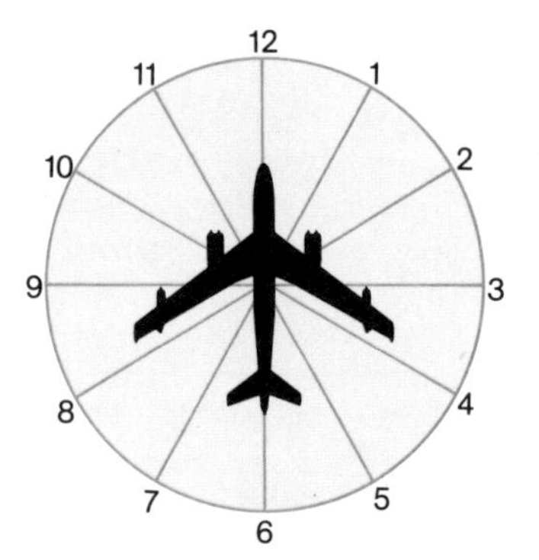

Major L. D. Chase was skipper of an RB-47 aircraft that took off from Forbes Air Force Base, Topeka, Kansas, on a training flight on the night of 19 September 1957. The RB-47 was a photo-reconnaissance version of the six-jet Boeing B-47 bomber. It was also equipped for electronic counter-measures (ECM), including location of enemy ground-based radar units, and identification of the systems employed, such as carrier frequency, pulse rate and width, scan speed and bearing.

The mission of 19 September involved gunnery exercises and navigation over the Gulf of Mexico, and an ECM exercise over the southern central United States. In addition to the skipper, there were a co-pilot, a navigator and three officers manning the three ECM monitors on board. Number 1 monitor was a direction-finding system with antennae on permanent mountings on the wing-tips. Number 2 monitor employed back-to-back antennae spinning in a housing beneath the rear fuselage of the plane, and the signals from this array were processed in a radar receiver and a pulse analyser. Number 3 monitor was not involved in the night's extraordinary events.

On the return trip from the Gulf of Mexico, the RB-47 crossed the Mississippi coastline near Gulfport and headed for Jackson, Mississippi, where the ECM exercise was to begin, at more than 30,000 feet (9000 metres) and at a speed of 500 knots (900 km/h). It was then that Captain McClure on No 2 monitor picked up an unexpected signal. The radar-scope was showing a signal at 5 o'clock, which meant a signal source behind them to starboard and out over the sea. Captain McClure assumed that the traces from the two antennae of the monitor had somehow switched and that the signal must actually be coming from a ground radar unit in Louisiana, at the 11 o'clock position. Indeed, the signal he was receiving checked out at a frequency of 2800 megahertz, a band commonly used for search radars. The lobe continued to show a 'blip' moving upscope to 4 o'clock, then to 3 o'clock and so on, but when it passed 12 o'clock and continued downscope, Captain McClure realised that the signal must be correct. But what could it be coming from?

The RB-47 changed course at Jackson and headed westwards towards Fort Worth and Dallas. Suddenly the pilots saw a white light in front of them; the crew was warned to expect evasive action, but before anything could happen the light hurtled across from left to right in front of the aeroplane.

Captain McClure heard the pilots discussing the light over the intercom, and told them of the signal that had puzzled him earlier. He then tuned No 2 monitor to 2800

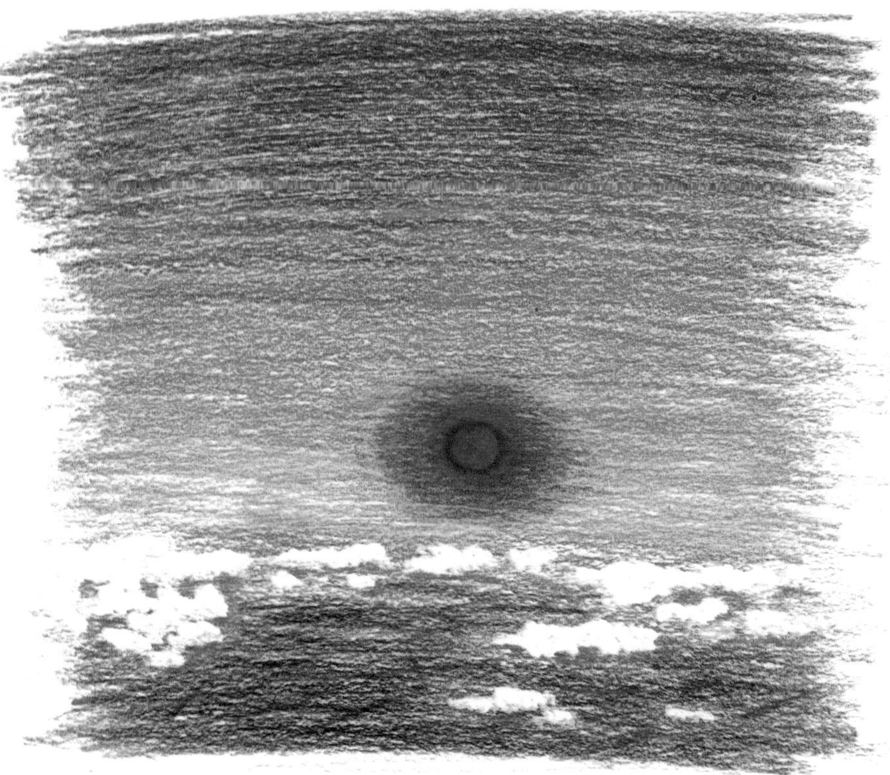

kilohertz, and instantly picked up a strong signal at the 2 o'clock position. The signal did not move downscope; this showed that the source maintained a constant position relative to the aircraft.

After the RB-47 had been 'escorted' by the UFO for more than 100 miles (160 kilometres), the skipper called up Carswell Air Force Base, where a Ground Control Intercept (GCI) radar was in operation. Number 1 monitor had by now confirmed the existence of a target at the 2 o'clock position. Carswell came back with the information that there was another aircraft 10 miles (16 kilometres) from the RB-47 at 2 o'clock.

Captain McClure thereupon realised that the blip that had puzzled him had been a true reading of an unknown signal source, which was circling the RB-47 in flight!

The UFO now moved forward, detected as it did so by both the GCI at Carswell and the No 2 monitor on the aeroplane, and when it reached the 12 o'clock position both pilots could actually see it, glowing red and 'bigger than a house.'

Between Fort Worth and Dallas, the UFO changed course, and Major Chase obtained permission to follow it. He immediately found that the aircraft was closing on the object – which was simultaneously reported by GCI to be stationary. At that point, the light blinked out and the traces of the unknown object disappeared from the radar-scopes. Major Chase put the RB-47 into a left turn, and the light suddenly reappeared at a lower level – probably about 15,000 feet (4500 metres) – and its trace returned to the radar-scopes. The skipper was given permission to dive his aircraft towards the object, and he took it down to 20,000 feet (6000 metres) before the light blinked out again, and the signal on the radar at GCI at Carswell disappeared.

The RB-47 now climbed to 25,000 feet (7600 metres) and headed for Oklahoma; its fuel was running low. Once again, according to Carswell GCI, the UFO re-appeared and followed 10 miles (16 kilometres) behind the aeroplane, into southern Oklahoma, where it finally disappeared. In all this, the UFO had stayed with the aircraft for more than an hour, during which time a distance of more than 800 miles (1250 kilometres) was covered.

The incident was immediately investigated by officers from White Sands Missile Base, from Kirtland Air Force Base, and from Project Blue Book at Wright Patterson Air Force Base. Dr J. Allen Hynek was also present. But, despite the efforts of all the experts, two questions remain unsolved: was the unidentified object under intelligent control? And if so, who was controlling it?

'Threads of the Virgin'

Daylight disc: Oloron-Sainte-Marie, France, 17 October 1952; Gaillac, France, 27 October 1952

At lunch-time on Friday 17 October 1952, a strange object appeared in the clear blue sky over Oloron-Sainte-Marie and nearby villages in the south-west of France. The headmaster of the lycée in Oloron-Sainte-Marie was at home at the time; looking out to the northern side of the town from his dining-room window, he saw a solitary cloud crossing the sky at an estimated altitude of 6500 to 9800 feet (2000 to 3000 metres). There was nothing unusual about this; but above the cloud, and travelling at the same speed, was an object shaped like a cylinder, white in colour, and not luminous, tilted at an angle of 45°. The upper part of this cylinder was leaning in the direction in which it was moving – towards the south-west – and puffs of white smoke, or cloud, seemed to be detaching themselves from the top. Ahead of the cylinder, and travelling in the same direction, were some 30 small objects that looked like balls of smoke.

Looking through his binoculars, the headmaster could see that each of these smaller objects consisted of a red central sphere, encircled by a yellow-hued ring inclined at such an angle that it hid much of the lower part of the sphere. Indeed, the objects appeared to be domed saucers, and they were moving about in pairs in swift zig-zag flight, with each pair linked by what looked like an electric arc.

A sort of side-phenomenon now became visible. The smaller objects left long trails of a threadlike substance, which detached itself and floated slowly earthwards. The threads festooned themselves about roofs, trees and walls, street lamps, telephone wires, cables and so on. The material – which the villagers immediately named 'threads of the Virgin' – looked like strands of nylon, or finely-spun wool. When touched it became gelatinous, then vaporised and disappeared.

This phenomenon within a phenomenon, which is rare indeed, is known in English-speaking circles as 'angel hair'.

Sceptics were stumped by the 'show' at Oloron-Sainte-Marie: since so many people over a wide area had seen the same thing, it could hardly be dismissed as an hallucination. However, genuine 'threads of the Virgin' are left by spiders, and it was suggested that the festoons of filigree-like thread had been left by millions of migrating spiders. This explanation, however, did not account for the fact that, unlike spider threads, the 'angel hair' at Oloron-Sainte-Marie disintegrated within a few minutes.

The furore had almost died down when, on 27 October, at least 100 residents of Gaillac, also in south-west France – including two NCOs of the Gendarmerie – saw a repeat performance of the events at Oloron-Sainte-Marie. The time was 5 p.m., and the only difference reported between the phenomena was that there were 20 small saucers, which came much closer to the ground during their zig-zag manoeuvres, their minimum altitude being about 1300 feet (400 metres). On this occasion, the witnesses likened the falling threads to glass wool. The 'angel hair' was still falling and slowly vaporising long after the cylinder and saucers had passed out of sight to the south-east.

What was the purpose of the twin UFO displays at Oloron-Sainte-Marie and Gaillac? Nothing quite like them has ever been seen again. It is tempting to think that these spectaculars were put on for the benefit of humans by whatever it is that controls the UFO phenomenon – perhaps as a kind of announcement of the period of intense UFO activity that began in 1954.

Below right: 'angel hair' similar to that found after the Oloron-Sainte-Marie and Gaillac sightings. The filigree-like strands became gelatinous, disintegrated and vaporised within a few minutes

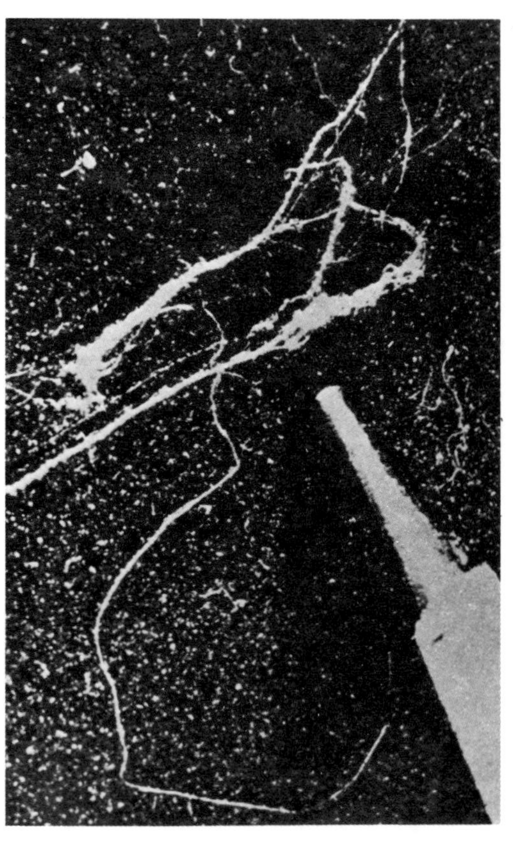

Encounters in the air

ONLY RARELY do we hear of UFO sightings involving airmen, especially military ones, for the good reason that governments have no wish to foster the notion that national defence is in the hands of eccentrics. But another view may be taken of such sightings: that the very reliability of the witnesses should speak for the reality of the phenomenon. Yet governments persist in maintaining a public silence – while, at the same time, taking careful note of unusual or inexplicable events in the air.

'Surprise turned to horror'

Close encounter of the first kind: Southend-on-Sea, Essex, England 14 October 1954

On 14 October 1954, Flight-Lieutenant James R. Salandin, flying a Meteor twin-jet fighter plane, narrowly avoided collision with an unidentified flying object over Southend-on-Sea, Essex.

What happened next was told to Derek Dempster, the then editor of *Flying Saucer Review*, and the story appeared in the very first issue of the magazine. (Derek Dempster was himself an ex-RAF pilot and knew how pilots value their professional reputation. Sensation seeking is not their style.)

Above: a Gloster Meteor Mark 8 fighter. From 1950 to 1958 this aircraft was the main daylight interceptor used by the RAF. Flight-Lieutenant James Salandin flew one as part of a nationwide air defence network designed – in the days before intercontinental ballistic missiles – to prevent enemy bombers reaching British targets

Jimmy Salandin was one of the 'weekend' pilots of No. 604 County of Middlesex Squadron, Royal Auxiliary Air Force. He had reported for duty at North Weald, Essex, on the afternoon of 14 October, and at 4.15 p.m. took off in his Meteor Mark 8 jet. Climbing southwards into a blue and cloudless sky he soon observed two other Meteors flying in formation high above him and leaving long vapour trails. Flight-Lieutenant Salandin watched the passage of the two aircraft while occasionally checking his instruments.

He had reached 16,000 feet (4880 metres) over the outlying districts of Southend, when to his surprise he saw two circular objects, travelling in the opposite direction to the Meteors, hurtle between them. One of the objects was silvery in colour, the other gold. Salandin watched them until they disappeared, at the '9 o'clock high' position – to his port, or left, side.

After checking his own instruments he turned his gaze to the air in front of him. His surprise turned to horror – for he saw a

silvery object streaking straight towards him.

For a few split seconds he saw a thing that 'had a bun-shaped top, a flange like two saucers in the middle, and a bun underneath . . . it could not have been far off because it overlapped the windscreen'. (Derek Dempster noted that a Meteor's 37-foot [11-metre] wing span just fills the windscreen at 150 yards [140 metres].) The flying saucer, which was travelling at tremendous speed, avoided a head-on collision at the very last second by suddenly swerving off past the jet on its port side.

Badly shaken, the Flight-Lieutenant flew around quietly for 10 minutes or so to regain his composure, and reported his experience to ground control. He was annoyed, too, when he realised later that his camera – standard equipment on combat aircraft – had been loaded all the time. With everything happening so quickly he didn't have time to press the button. A valuable opportunity to gather evidence for ufology had been missed.

'Coming for me right now'

Close encounter of the second kind: Bass Strait, Australia
21 October 1978

When a Cessna 182 light aircraft, owned by Southern Air Services of Moorabbin, in Melbourne, Australia, went missing on the evening of Saturday, 21 October 1978, when flying over Bass Strait, emergency measures were set in motion; light aircraft and a marine reconnaissance plane began a search. It seemed straightforward enough – a tragic accident. The passage of time would fill in the details . . . But within 24 hours that situation had begun to change when the words 'unidentified flying object' were whispered here and there in connection with the incident. And in another 12 hours the Australian press was scrambling to print the story with banner headlines on Monday, 23 October. The sensational account swept from continent to continent; for example it was featured in a breakfast-time radio news flash that same day in Philadelphia, USA.

The lone pilot was Frederick Valentich, aged 20, of Avondale Heights, Melbourne. He had held an unrestricted flying licence for only nine months but was considered a competent pilot and was held in high esteem by his colleagues. He had been flying to King Island, midway between Cape Otway, Victoria, and Tasmania, where he was to collect crayfish for the officers' mess of the Air Training Corps – of which he was an instructor – but it was primarily an excuse for him to log up some night-flying time. (Although he had made the trip several times in daylight, this was the first time he had flown it after dark.) It was his intention to be back in Melbourne by 10.00 p.m.

Valentich took off in the Cessna at 6.19 p.m. and flew over Cape Otway, where there is a lighthouse, at about 7.00 p.m. There was a north-westerly breeze and visibility was excellent. At 7.06 p.m. he contacted ground

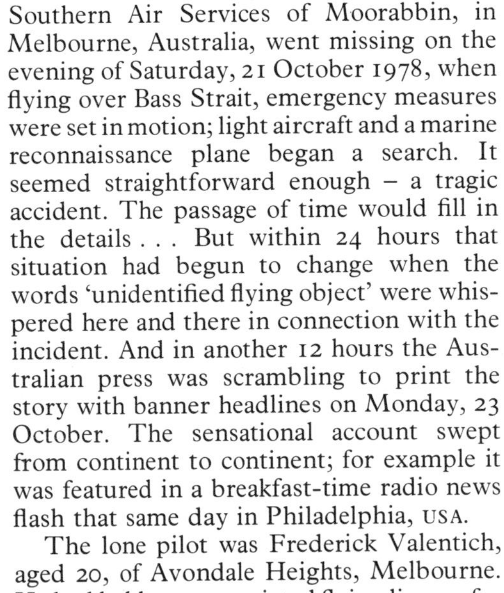

Below: a Cessna 182 like the one flown by Frederick Valentich. A best-seller in its class, the 182 is renowned as a rugged, reliable workhorse

control at Melbourne Flight Service. Parts of the Flight Service transcript of the ensuing conversation appeared in Australian newspapers, including the *Sun* and the *Australian*, on the morning of 23 October:

7.06 p.m.

Pilot: Is there any known traffic in my area below 5000 feet [1500 metres].

Flight Service Unit: Negative. No known traffic.

Pilot: Seems to be a large aircraft below 5000 feet [1500 metres].

FSU: What type of aircraft?

Pilot: I cannot confirm. It has four bright lights that appear to be landing lights . . . aircraft has just passed over me, about 1000 feet [300 metres] above.

FSU: Is large aircraft confirmed?

Pilot: Affirmative, at speed it is travelling.

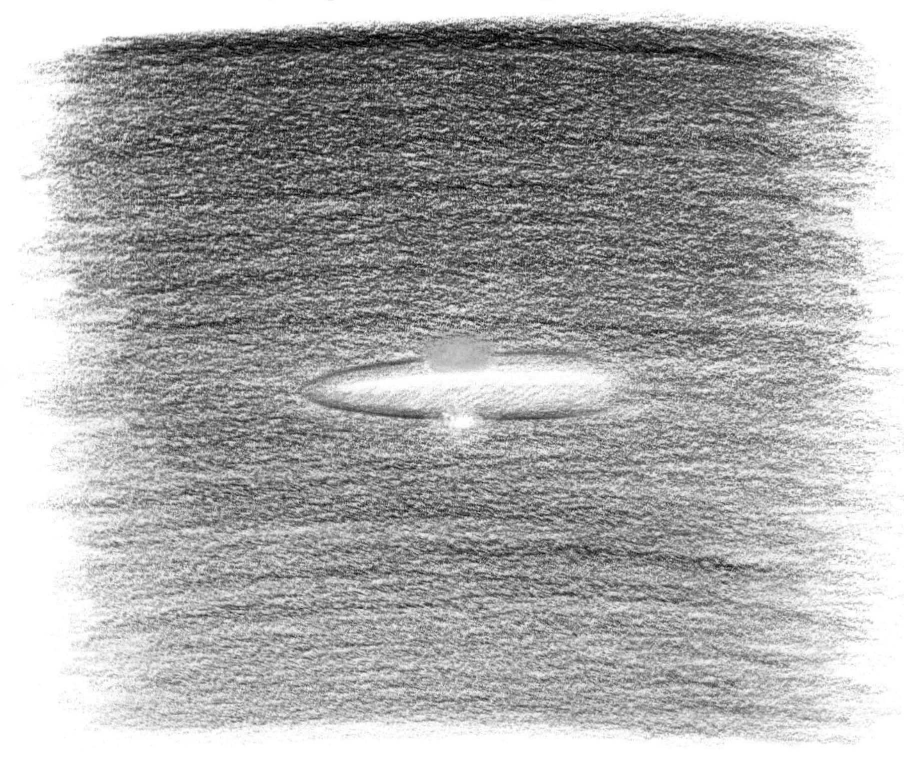

Are there any RAAF aircraft in the vicinity?

FSU: Negative.

7.08 p.m.

Pilot: Melbourne, it's approaching from due east of me. It seems to be playing some sort of game. Flying at speed I can't estimate.

FSU: What is your altitude?

Pilot: 4500 feet [1400 metres].

7.09 p.m.

FSU: Can you confirm you cannot identify the aircraft?

Pilot: Affirmative. It's not an aircraft. It's . . . (Break in transmission)

FSU: Can you describe aircraft?

Pilot: It's flying past. It has a long shape. Cannot identify more than that . . . coming for me right now. It seems to be stationary. I'm orbiting and the thing is orbiting on top of me. It has a green light and a sort of metallic light on the outside.

Valentich then told ground control that the object seemed to have vanished. Control followed by advising him that there were no military aircraft in the area.

7.12 p.m.

Pilot: Engine is rough-idling and coughing.

FSU: What are your intentions?

Pilot: Proceeding King Island . . . unknown aircraft now on top of me.

FSU: Acknowledge.

There followed a long 'metallic' noise, and thereafter contact with the Cessna was lost.

When the plane failed to arrive at King Island at the expected time of 7.28 p.m. the visual and radio search began. The Cessna had been equipped with the standard life jacket and a radio survival beacon, but no sound was ever traced from it. An RAAF Orion from Edinburgh, South Australia, conducted its 'tracking crawl' on 22 and 23 October; and reported only an oil-slick north of King Island.

Borrowed by the aliens?

There were several attempts to explain away the alleged UFO connection. It was suggested that the pilot might have become disorientated and had managed to invert his aircraft so that the lights he saw, and thought were those of the UFO, were in fact reflections of his own aircraft's lights on the sea, or were perhaps from the lighthouses at Cape Otway or King Island. Experienced pilots stated publicly, however, that such an explanation was as extraordinary as the reported UFO encounter, for there was the recorded six-minute radio conversation during which the lights were mentioned more than once, and that type of aircraft could only be flown for about 30 seconds upside down before the engine would stop from fuel starvation.

From interviews on 23 October it seemed that the pilot's father sought solace from flying saucer 'enthusiasts' and their theories. Mr Guido Valentich stated that his son was a 'believer' in UFOs, and had 'read a lot on the subject'. He was even reported as believing that his son had been 'borrowed by interplanetary visitors' – a hope that was preferable to the thought that he had lost his son in the depths of the sea.

Australian investigator Bill Chalker, writing in *Flying Saucer Review*, pointed out that Frederick Valentich was a person who 'lived for flying' and was hardly likely to have made wild claims that would have affected his professional reputation as a pilot and his chances of promotion.

So possible explanations are that he did encounter a UFO and in his final excitement and turmoil crashed, without trace, into the sea; that he collided with a UFO with the same result; or that he perpetrated a hoax. Concluded Chalker: 'This [last hypothesis] must be a consideration if Frederick Valentich turns up alive and well, but as time passes the possibility becomes increasingly less likely.'

UFO Photo File

At about 7.45 p.m. on 11 May 1950 at his farm close by the Salmon River Highway, about 10 miles south-west of McMinnville, Oregon. Paul Trent and his wife claimed they saw a UFO – and took a photograph of it which has still not been proved a fake.

Mrs Trent was in the yard on the south side of the house feeding the rabbits when she saw, to the north-east, moving westwards, a disc-shaped object. She called her husband, who was inside the house. When he realised the unusual nature of the object in the sky, Mr Trent ran to his car for his camera, but his wife remembered that he had left it in the house and hurried to fetch it. The camera already had a partly used film in it.

The object was tilted up a little as it approached, and appeared bright and silvery; it made no noise, and the Trents saw no smoke or vapour. Mr Trent took a picture (*above*) and wound on ready for the next frame, moving to the right to keep the object in the viewfinder, and taking a second shot some 30 seconds after the first. Mrs Trent said the object seemed to be gliding, with no rotating or undulating motion. It moved off westwards and 'dimly vanished'.

The couple said there was a 'breeze' as the object tilted before flying overhead. Mr Trent estimated its diameter as 20 or 30 feet (6 or 9 metres).

A few days later, when he had used up the remaining frames, Mr Trent had the film developed locally. He mentioned the incident to only a few friends. He did not seek publicity, telling his friends he didn't want to be 'in trouble with the government'. However, a reporter from the local *McMinnville Telephone Register* heard of the sighting from two of Mr Trent's friends; he followed it up and found the precious negatives on the floor of the Trents' house, under a writing desk where the Trent children had been playing with them! The *Telephone Register's* story appeared on 8 June 1950. On 9 and 10 June newspapers in Portland, Oregon, and in Los Angeles ran the story, and *Life* magazine carried the photographs a week later.

None of this publicity had been sought by the Trents. When, 17 years after the sighting, they were visited by an investigator from the US Air Force-sponsored Colorado University Commission of Enquiry (whose findings were later published as the Condon Report) he found them completely unchanged by their experience, well liked locally and known as reliable.

The McMinnville UFO (above left) is remarkable for its similarity to an object (above right) seen and photographed from an aeroplane by a French Air Marshal near Rouen, France, in March 1954.

After submitting the photographs to rigorous scientific examination the Condon investigation was forced to admit they might be genuine. The official report concluded: 'This is one of the few UFO reports in which all factors investigated, geometric, psychological and physical appear to be consistent.'

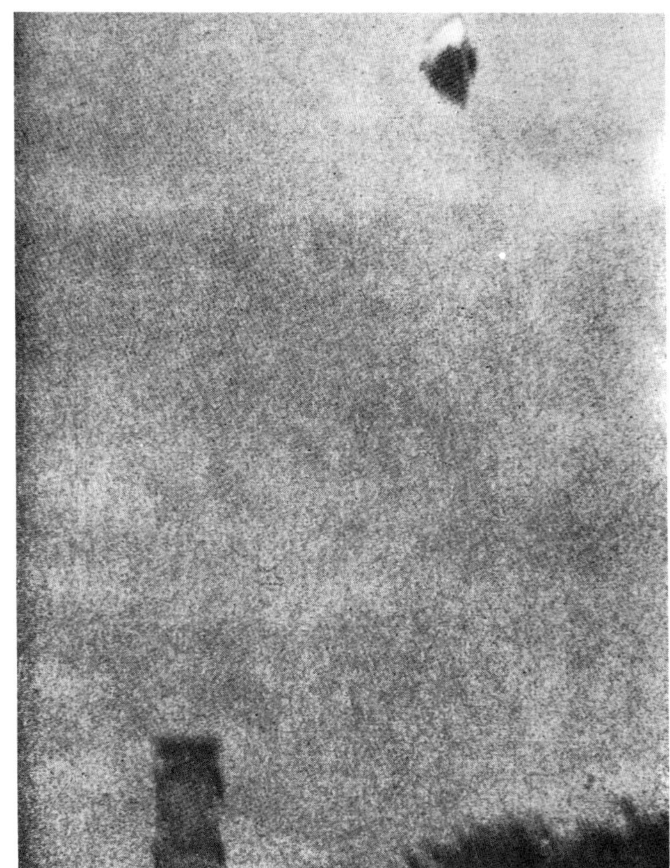

One warm, clear afternoon in early April 1966, Mr Brown (he wishes his real name to remain secret) was in his garden in Balwyn, near Melbourne, Australia, when it suddenly 'lit up' and he saw in the sky a bright object, shaped like a mushroom (left), about 20 to 35 feet (6 to 10 metres) in diameter. It was about 150 feet (50 metres) from the ground and seemed to float down towards him, spinning through a 180° angle on its vertical axis, 'during which time I photographed it'. It then shot off northwards at high speed. A carpenter working in the house witnessed the object and saw Brown photograph it.

Mr Brown is a qualified engineer, director of a large family business, and is a respected citizen of Balwyn. It is difficult to believe he would perpetrate a hoax. And yet an American UFO organisation, Ground Saucer Watch Inc., of Phoenix, Arizona, has recently cast doubt on the authenticity of the photograph. Using computer techniques to analyse the photograph, GSW has claimed it is a fake. And yet GSW has often been wrong in the past. Who is right? It is a question that is impossible to answer.

A promotional photograph of a B-57 aeroplane in flight (below) found its way into a set of UFO photographs offered for sale by NICAP (National Investigations Committee on Aerial Phenomena). An unknown object appeared in the top right-hand corner of the photograph. According to UFO investigator Robert Schmidt, the object 'appeared to be streamlined, and to have dark "ports" on its lower periphery.'

Schmidt wrote to the manufacturers, the Martin Aircraft Company, asking for a bigger enlargement (inset left) from the NICAP file. When questioned about the picture, the company replied that the unexplained image had been caused by a tear, a rub or an abrasion. Analysis, however, subsequently showed that in the original negative the emulsion grain extended over the area of the unknown object; a tear or rub would have destroyed the grain.

The Martin Company also said they had filmed another 'fly-by' to see if the same effect could be obtained again – a strange thing to do if, as they claimed, the original image had been caused by a flaw in the film.

Sightings and side effects

THE 'REALITY' OF UFOS – whether they are 'nuts and bolts' craft, or some vision-like projection – is the subject of hot debate. But witnesses and participants in close encounters frequently report physical side-effects such as violent headaches, fits of weeping, and buzzing in the ears. In the cases that follow, zoo animals stampede and soldiers are paralysed in Malagasy while an Argentinian girl weeps for days after a UFO passes by – so just how 'unreal' can such alien craft actually be?

'A luminous green ball'

Close encounter of the second kind: Tananarive, Madagascar, August 1954

One of the most spectacular of all 'light in the sky' UFO fly-overs took place over the city of Tananarive, capital of Madagascar (now Malagasy) one day in August 1954.

Edmond Campagnac, head of Technical Services of Air France, was waiting with a group of people outside the Air France office on the Avenue de la Libération for the arrival of the air mail from Paris.

Suddenly Monsieur Campagnac saw a luminous green ball in the sky. It was descending, almost vertically, like a meteorite. Other people followed his gaze, and the object was seen to disappear behind mountains to the south of the city.

The time was 5.45 p.m. and dusk was approaching, although the setting Sun was still visible. While the group waited outside the Air France office, they were joined by scores of others on the streets as people began their journeys home from work.

The witnesses were still watching when an object of the same colour as that seen seconds earlier appeared over the hills near the old Queen's Palace, this time 'flying' horizontally and at a slower speed. The UFO curved past the government buildings, still appearing like a green ball. Soon it was descending even lower, almost to roof-top height, and heading along the eastern side of the Avenue de la Libération, just above the building opposite the Air France office.

As the light drew level with the group, they saw that it was in fact *two* objects. A lentil-shaped device was leading the way, and this was described as having the colour of an 'electric-green luminous gas'. Following some 100 feet (30 metres) behind was a metallic-looking cylindrical object, about 130 feet (40 metres) in length. While described by some as a 'cigar', others said it looked more like the fuselage of the contemporary Constellation aircraft shorn of fins, elevators, wings and engines. The surface of the cylinder reflected the dying rays of the sun, while behind it there splayed a plume of orange-red flame. Estimates of the speed of the objects were in the region of 300 km/h (185 miles per hour).

People stopped and gazed in amazement at the phenomenon, so much so that a pall of quietness hung over the city. The giant cigar and its lenticular companion were completely silent. Then there was another shock for the observers for, as the objects passed over the buildings, all the electric lights were extinguished, coming on again only after the objects had passed.

The strange aerial duo continued over the city towards Tananarive airport, then swung away to the west. Before passing from sight they skimmed over a zoological park where the animals, which were normally quite undisturbed by aircraft flying into and out of the airport, went into a panic and stampeded through fences. It was several hours before soldiers and police could round them up.

Not surprisingly there was a great furore in Tananarive over this invasion of Madagascan airspace, and an official enquiry was set up by General Fleurquin, the Air Force Commandant. This was conducted by Father Coze, director of the Tananarive Observatory. Father Coze had been at the observatory at the time of the incident and had himself witnessed the passage of the UFOs. He estimated that at least 20,000 people had seen the objects, and he and his helpers questioned more than 5000 witnesses. It is not known what happened to his report of this remarkable encounter. If it ever reached France, it certainly failed to arouse interest. Details were known only to a handful of French researchers in the early 1960s,

and to *Flying Saucer Review* in 1966, which received an account from Monsieur René Fouéré of the *Groupement d'Etude de Phénomènes Aeriens* (GEPA). But not a hint of the affair was known to the French public until 1974, when M. Jean-Claude Bourret broadcast his famous series of programmes on Radio France-Inter, transcripts of which appeared in his book *The crack in the Universe*, published in 1977.

'A shining egg'

Close encounter of the second kind: Malagasy Republic, May 1967

In May 1967 there was said to be another alarming close encounter in Malagasy. But it took 10 years before news of the incident reached *Flying Saucer Review* from the French research group *Lumières dans la nuit*. On this occasion, the reason for the delay was that the witnesses were 23 soldiers, their officer and four NCOs of the French Foreign Legion, and they were forbidden to discuss the affair. The eventual informant was a legionnaire named Wolff.

Wolff's platoon, which was on a reconnaissance exercise, had halted at noon in a clearing in the bush country. The troops were eating lunch when they all saw a bright metallic object resembling a 'shining egg' descend rapidly like a falling leaf, accompanied by a piercing, whistling sound, then thump into the ground. All the soldiers were 'paralysed' and, seemingly immediately, saw the object take off. But when watches were checked, the time was 3.15 p.m., which meant that three hours had passed.

M. Wolff claimed that the object was about 23 feet (7 metres) high and 10 to 13 feet (3 to 4 metres) wide at the widest part. It rose slowly at first, and then vanished at high speed, as though 'sucked up into the sky'. It left three marks in the ground that looked as if they had been made by legs, and a 10-foot (3-metre) deep crater, at the bottom of which was a sort of vitrified ring of coloured crystals.

None of the witnesses could recall what had happened during the missing hours, but for two days afterwards they all had violent headaches, with constant 'beating' in the region of the temples and a continual buzzing sound in the ears.

'An impression of goodness and kindness'

Close encounter of the third kind: Córdoba, Argentina, June 1968

The Motel La Cuesta is a well-appointed roadhouse, situated on Highway 20 that connects the town of Villa Carlos Paz, in the province of Córdoba, with eastern Argentina. The small country town is 500 miles (800 kilometres) to the west of Buenos Aires.

The motel's proprietor, Señor Pedro Pretzel, 39, lived at the motel with his wife and his 19-year-old daughter, Maria Eladia.

On the night of 13 June 1968, at about 12.50 a.m., Señor Pretzel was walking home when he saw, some 55 yards (50 metres) beyond the motel – and apparently on the highway – an object that he could not identify. It had two bright red lights, but could not be a car because it projected beams of peculiar intensity at the motel. This 'machine' was in view for only a few seconds. Puzzled and alarmed, Señor Pretzel ran to his motel and found Maria Eladia lying in a dead faint close to the kitchen door. After she had been revived she had a bizarre tale to tell.

Only a few minutes earlier she had said goodnight to her fiancé and had escorted some guests to the door; then she returned to the kitchen. Suddenly she noticed that the lobby was flooded with light. As she had just switched the lights off, she went to investigate. She was horrified to find herself face-to-face with a 'man' some 6 feet (2 metres) tall, dressed in a kind of diver's suit that had shiny, sky-blue scales. He was fair-haired, and was holding up his left hand, on the palm of which a sky-blue ball, or sphere, was moving about.

Maria said there was a huge ring on the fourth finger of the creature's right hand, which he moved up and down constantly in front of her. She was overcome by lethargy, as though strength was being drained from her. Light came from the creature's fingertips and feet and it seemed to Maria that the lethargic feeling was strongest when the light was pointed directly at her. But apart from this he showed no signs of aggression. Indeed, Maria remembers an impression of 'goodness and kindness' emanating from the being who, she added, smiled throughout the encounter. She said he also seemed to be trying to communicate with her, for, although his lips did not move, she could hear an unintelligible mumble that sounded 'like Chinese'.

After a few minutes – during which Maria stood transfixed in the presence of the humanoid – he walked, with slow, precise movements, to the side door, which was open. He went out and the door closed of its own accord. It was at that moment that Maria lost consciousness. Shortly afterwards her father discovered her on the floor.

Señor Pretzel reported the incident to the police, who promised to investigate it. As for Maria, she became extremely nervous and was subject to fits of weeping for some days after the affair.

Did Maria Eladia Pretzel witness a projected image – that of a 'man' in her kitchen – that was emitted from the UFO her father had seen on the nearby highway? If she had been witness to such a phenomenon, then it is possible that her father came on the scene just as the image was about to be withdrawn. Could the 'humanoid' have been a hologram transmitted by laser beams and projected against, say, the glass of the lobby window? (The intense beams of light seemed to have been emitted by the UFO, and it was presumably this light that first attracted Maria's attention.)

But however the strange and alarming effects were produced the questions remain: Why? And by whom?

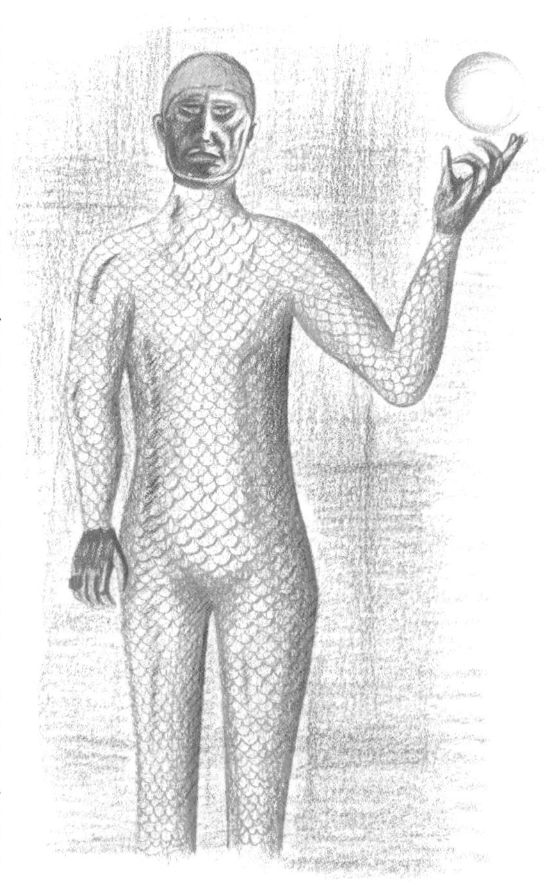

A meeting in Mendoza

FROM TIME TO TIME a bizarre UFO encounter is reported in which the witness, thanks either to his spontaneity or to his personal reaction, conveys an impression of credibility. Interest builds up around the case, only to be dashed by a confession that the whole thing has been a hoax. This can be so sudden that investigators into the case should consider whether undue pressure has been brought to bear on the witness to prompt such a recantation.

The strange experience of Fernando José Villegas and Juan Carlos Peccinetti of Mendoza in Argentina, is a case in point. Their immediate reactions to the nightmarish events that they claimed overtook them on 1 September 1968 certainly did not convey the impression that they were joking, yet in a matter of days they had 'confessed' that the story was false. How far was their retraction influenced by the fact that, at the time, the Mendoza authorities were threatening legal action against anyone reporting a UFO incident?

'Do not fear, do not fear'

Close encounter of the third kind: Mendoza, Argentina, 1 September 1968

At 3.30 a.m. on 1 September 1968, Juan Carlos Peccinetti and Fernando José Villegas, cashiers at a casino in Mendoza, Argentina, left work and set off for home in Villegas's vintage Chevrolet. They had just reached an unlighted part of the calle Nequén, near the junction with the calle Laprida, when the car suddenly stopped and the headlights went out. Villegas got out of the car to look under the bonnet.

At 4 a.m. soldiers on duty at the General Espejo Military College were startled when two young men burst into the guardroom in a state of shock, babbling that they had seen a flying saucer close to the ground. They claimed to have encountered five small beings, who communicated with them in a strange manner, took blood samples from their fingers, left inscriptions on their car, then returned to the flying saucer along a beam of light. The saucer then took off vertically at high speed and disappeared.

The soldiers insisted that the casino men should go to the Lagomagiore Hospital, which they did; the police were called in soon afterwards. The media were quickly on the trail and reports of the strange encounter appeared in *Los Principios* (2 September 1968), *Gente y la Actualidad* (5 September) and *La Crónica* (9 September). This is what is stated to have happened:

When Villegas got out of the car he cried out: 'Look, Skinny', and thereupon found himself unable to move. The same happened to Peccinetti as he scrambled out – the word 'paralysed' was used in the reports – and he found later that his watch had stopped at 3.42 a.m. (Villegas had no watch.) They found themselves facing three small beings, and two more were standing near a circular 'machine', some 13 feet (4 metres) across and 5 feet (1.5 metres) high, which was floating in

Right: Fernando José Villegas and Juan Carlos Peccinetti (far right), the two casino cashiers who felt obliged to confess that their reported encounter with ufonauts was a hoax. There were two versions of their retraction: one was that the cashiers themselves were the hoaxers; the other that someone else was responsible

These curious scratches on the side of Villegas's vintage Chevrolet were allegedly made by a humanoid with a device like a soldering iron

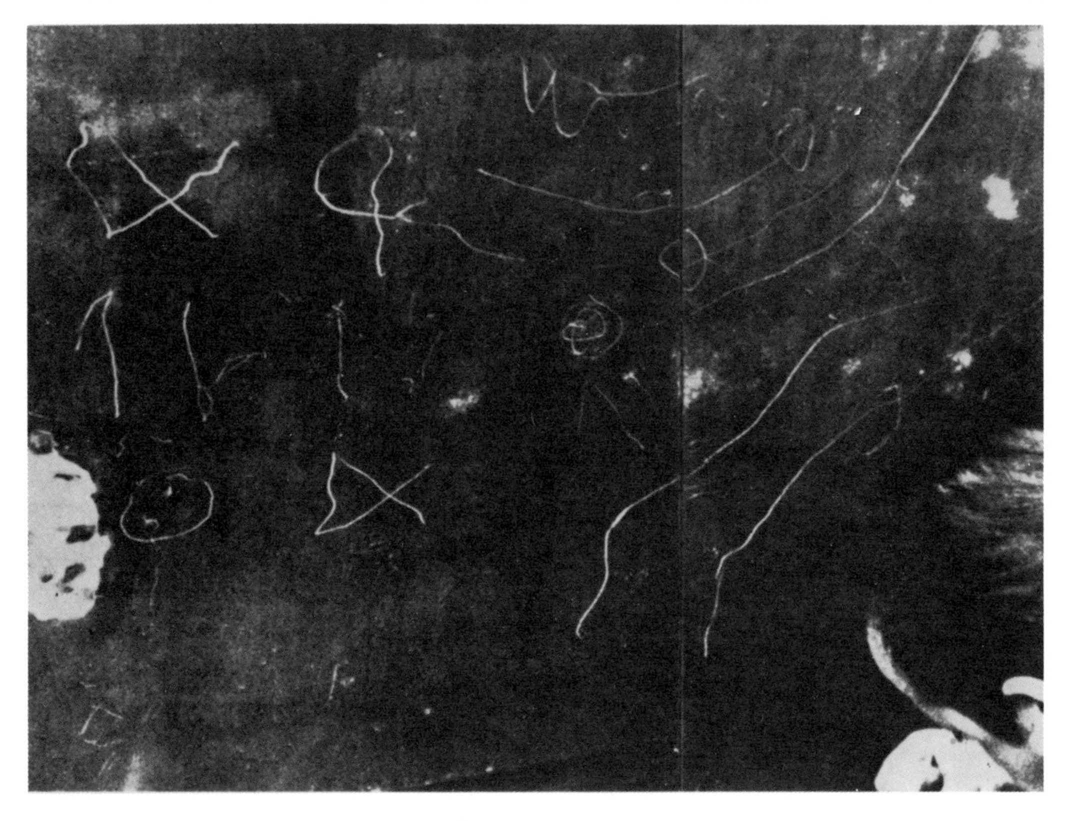

the air about 4 feet (1.2 metres) above a patch of the waste ground at 2333 calle Nequén. A beam of light was directed from the object towards the ground at an angle of about 45°.

The beings were said to be about 5 feet (1.5 metres) tall, and looked like humans but had unusually large heads, which were hairless. They were wearing boiler suits, and approached the alarmed cashiers 'gently and quietly', crossing a ditch 'as though by a bridge'. Both witnesses told how they heard – as though by the tiny earplugs from pocket transistor radios – a voice in Spanish saying repeatedly: 'Do not fear, do not fear.' Villegas also alleged that they had received a message in the same way; the gist of it was that the entities had just made three journeys around the Sun, studying the customs and languages of the inhabitants of the system; '. . . the Sun benignly nurtures the system: were it not so then the solar system would not exist. . . . Mathematics is the universal language.'

An investigator examines the inscriptions on the windscreen of the car

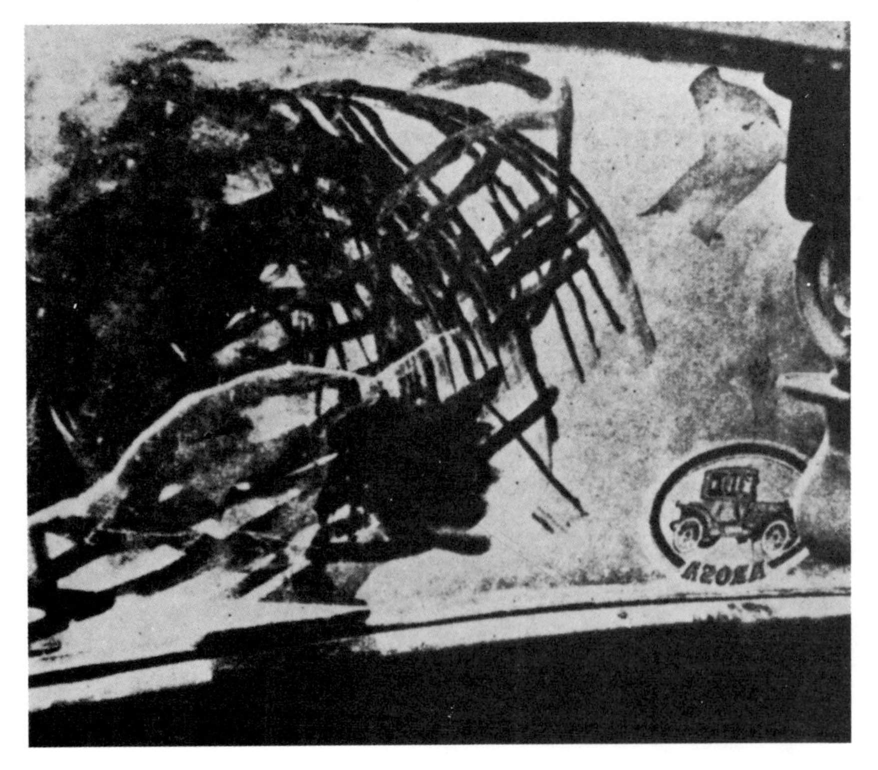

While this lecture proceeded, another of the entities was using an instrument like a soldering iron to make inscriptions on the doors, windscreen and running boards of the vintage car. There were bright sparks from the device, but when the car was examined later no burn marks were found.

A circular screen then appeared near the hovering object, and on it the two men saw a series of pictures. The first was a scene of a waterfall in lush countryside; the second showed a mushroom-shaped cloud, and the third the waterfall again, but neither water nor lushness. After this, said the witnesses, their left hands were taken by hands that felt no different from those of humans, and their fingers were pricked three times. The beings then retreated to their craft, ascending to it by way of the light beam. Then there was the sound of an explosion and, surrounded by intense light, the object rose into the sky and disappeared.

From the college guardroom, Peccinetti and Villegas went to the Lagomagiore Hospital, where they were examined. The report on them stated: 'Picture of psychomotor

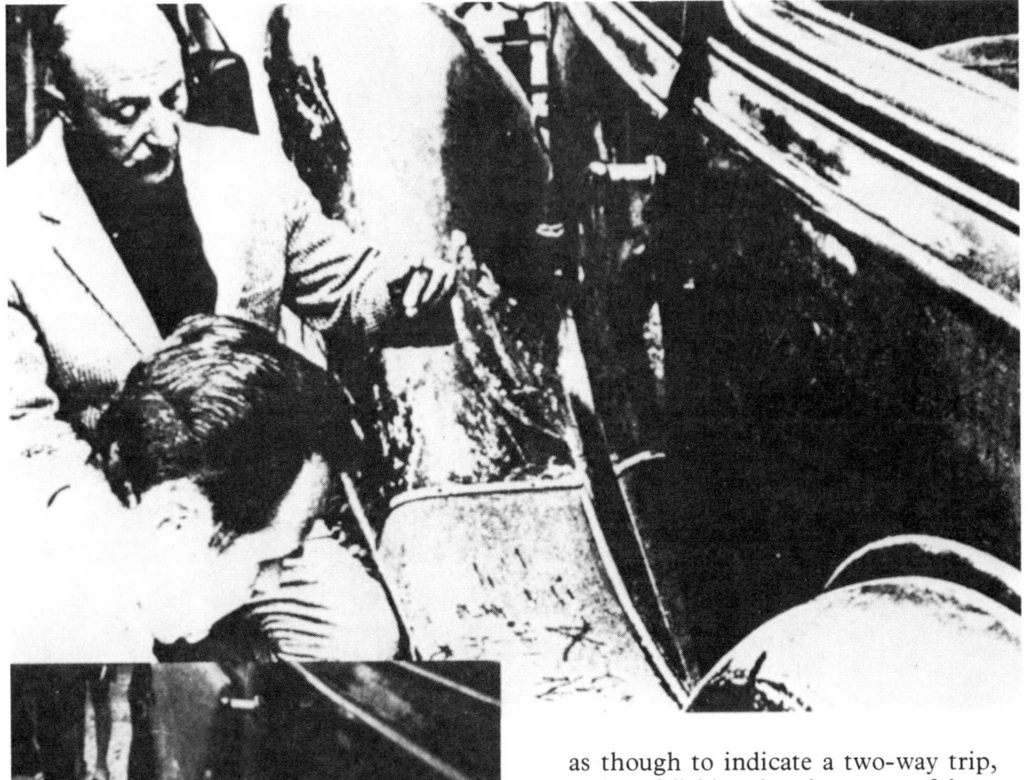

According to the proposal put forward by the Mendoza Centre for Space Research, the inscriptions on the car show that the entities encountered by Villegas and Peccinetti came from Ganymede, one of the moons of Jupiter

excitation and three small punctures on the flesh parts of the index and middle fingers of the left hand. Identical in both of them.'

Further tests were carried out at the Central Hospital, and the men were found to be sane and rational. The cashiers were kept apart for two days, during which time their stories tallied impressively.

The Chevrolet was impounded by the police and radioactivity tests on it revealed nothing abnormal. As for the inscriptions on the car, linguistics expert Gordon Creighton wrote to *Flying Saucer Review* that they seemed childishly unsystematic. The Mendoza Centre for Space Research, however, suggested that:

> The sketch done by the humanoids represents two solar systems, the Earth's system, consisting of Mercury, Venus and Earth, and the Jupiter system, containing the planets Io, Europa and Ganymede. Between Ganymede and Earth there are two parallel lines, as though to indicate a two-way trip, and establishing that the source of these beings is Ganymede.

As the platitudinous nature of the messages is typical of many alleged conversations with extra-terrestrials, Creighton's view of the script seems preferable. It is possible that the two cashiers did have a very real experience, triggered off by an object that was capable (perhaps electromagnetically, or by laser technology) of stopping the car; perhaps that object projected images for them to see, and hear, of entities, messages and cataclysmic warnings, and induced them unwittingly to scratch crude symbols on their car, and to prick their fingers.

There were some reports of possibly corroborating events – unknown at the time to the two witnesses, the college guards and the staff at the hospitals where the witnesses were examined. Staff at the Mendoza railway station had reported a sudden and total blackout of the lighting system at about 3.40 a.m., while at 3.45 a.m. Senora Maria Spinelli telephoned the police from her home in Dorrego, about 4 miles (6 kilometres) from the site of the encounter, to report that a strange luminous object was flying around very low overhead.

By 7 September 1968 notices began to appear in the Argentine press to the effect that 'the authorities have issued a communiqué that the spreading of saucer rumours is an offence penalized by law . . . that the penal code contemplates prison terms for people indulging in spreading unwarranted fear . . .' The authorities referred to were those of the Mendoza province; within days Peccinetti and Villegas took the easy way out and recanted.

UFO Photo File

Above: 'long object with hump on back' photographed over Bear Mountain in New York State by an anonymous witness on 18 December 1966. The sighting was reported to the US Air Force's Project Blue Book who took possession of the two photographs and a negative and interviewed the witness exhaustively. Although their own technicians could find no evidence of fraud the file was nevertheless labelled 'Hoax'. Doctor J. Allen Hynek wrote to Major Hector Quintanilla (then Chief of Project Blue Book) saying: '. . . the lack of satisfactory explanation of the unidentified object does not constitute sufficient reason to declare [it] a hoax. . . . My recommendation is . . . that the evaluation be changed from hoax to unidentified.' Despite this recommendation the 'Hoax' label remained. Why did the Air Force want to discredit the witness?

Below and below left: two frames from a film said to be of 'an approaching UFO', taken by Daniel W. Fry during May 1964 near his home in Merlin, Oregon, using a Bell and Howell movie camera. The UFO, described by Fry as 'spinning like a top during flight', was by no means the first he claimed to have encountered. It was, according to him, in 1950 that he witnessed his first 'saucer' landing, and during the next four years he became a contactee of 'the Space People'. They allegedly told him that they are the descendants of a lost super-race from Earth who survived a nuclear holocaust over 30,000 years ago and fled to live on Mars. Later they abandoned Mars and now live exclusively in their spacecraft. Fry is said to have taken a lie detector test on live television about his alleged contactee experiences and 'flunked it flat'.

Above right and right: another 'Martian spacecraft' photographed by Daniel W. Fry, also using a 16-millimetre Bell and Howell movie camera. The time is May 1965 and the place Joshua Tree, California. This craft is also described as 'spinning like a top' in the sky. Fry, an ex-employee of the Aerojet General Corporation (where he was 'in charge of installation of instruments for missile control and guidance'), is considered to be the most technically orientated of modern contactees. Sceptics may point out, however, that his uniquely technical background might provide him with opportunities to produce fake photographs of a high standard, but there is no conclusive evidence that these are fakes.

Two electrifying experiences

ONE OF THE CURIOSITIES of the history of UFOs is the clustering of UFO activity in which several incidents occur within a small locality only a few days apart. Sometimes the events are similar; sometimes – as in this pair of close encounters in south-east England – they appear to be linked only by place and time. But always there is a strange inconclusiveness about them, something that suggests that, if only we could find the missing link, we could understand what it is they are trying to tell us.

'About as big as a gasometer'

Close encounter of the second kind: Langenhoe, Essex, England, 14 September 1965

Early one Sunday morning – 14 September 1965 – at about one o'clock, an engineer named Paul Green, aged 29, was riding his motorcycle southwards along the B1025 road, which runs between Colchester and West Mersea in Essex. He had been visiting his fiancée, and was on his way home. The motorcycle was going well, purring along at some 40 miles per hour (70 km/h).

He had just passed through the village of Langenhoe, and was up to Pete Tye Common, when he overtook a rider on a motor scooter. A minute or so later he was approaching Langenhoe Hall when he heard a high-pitched humming noise away to his left – the east. As the noise became louder he looked up, expecting to see an approaching aeroplane, but saw only a small point of blue light about 5 miles (8 kilometres) away to the east, approximately over Brightlingsea.

As Paul Green watched the light winking, then growing brighter and flashing, he realised it was moving in his direction. Rapidly it became larger, and at the same time the humming became louder and louder. When the object was over Langenhoe Marsh he became uneasily aware that his motorcycle engine was coughing and spluttering, and after it had 'missed' several times, the engine stopped dead and the lights went off. At that point the flashing blue light was just over a mile (just under 2 kilometres) away, to the east of the road. Watching intently Paul now saw, within the extreme brightness of the light, an enormous object that resembled the upper half of a large spinning top – 'about as big as a gasometer' – with a dome on the upper part. The fierce blue flashes came from inside this dome. By now the object had stopped moving in his direction and, instead, was descending slowly, and at one stage tilting its underside towards him. The outer rim of this carried round objects spaced equidistantly so that it gave the impression of a 'luminous ball-race'.

Paul Green dismounted and took a few

involuntary steps towards the object, quickly coming to an unsteady halt. He later said, 'I felt spellbound and unable to move or speak, just as if I had become paralysed. The flashing blue light became so intense that it was painful, and it appeared to fluctuate in rhythm with my heart beat and hit against my chest. I felt myself tingling all over, rather like the electric shock one gets when handling an electrified cattle fence.'

At last the humming died down and the UFO descended towards the farmhouses at Wick. It was about then that the scooter that Paul had overtaken came coughing and spluttering to a halt. The rider, a young lad in a leather jacket, dismounted and stood looking at the flashing light as if transfixed. But Paul had no time to speak to him.

Paul reported: 'My head began to throb, and felt as though there were a band tightening around it. With a great effort I made myself move, and I grasped the bike and tried to start it.' In the end he managed to push it along, finally achieving a bump start, mounted and drove home as quickly as he could. After a short distance a line of tall hedges hid the 'thing' from him, but he could still see the blue glow in the sky.

It was unfortunate that the witness was so terrified by his encounter and the painful physiological effects that he never thought of speaking to the young man on the scooter; it meant that a chance of obtaining corroborative evidence was missed.

Paul Green arrived home at 2 a.m., and took the unusual course of awakening his invalid mother; he needed to tell someone of his experience. Next day his hair and clothes were so charged with static electricity that they crackled continually.

Two weeks after his frightening experience, Paul Green was interviewed for *Flying Saucer Review* by Dr Bernard Finch, one of its regular investigators. Dr Finch was convinced that Paul's story was true, and added that 'he described symptoms which can only be ascribed to the effects of a very powerful magnetic field on the human body.' He went on to speculate that, if this field were strong enough, it could produce a kind of light 'as yet unknown to our science'.

There is an interesting postscript to the story. A few days after the incident, Paul was discussing his experience with a friend who lived at nearby Shrub End, some 5 miles (8 kilometres) north-west of Langenhoe. He told Paul that, around the time Paul saw the UFO, he was at home when suddenly his dog started to bark. He opened the door to let the dog out – and saw a large blue light passing rapidly by in the sky directly overhead; it was travelling towards the north-west.

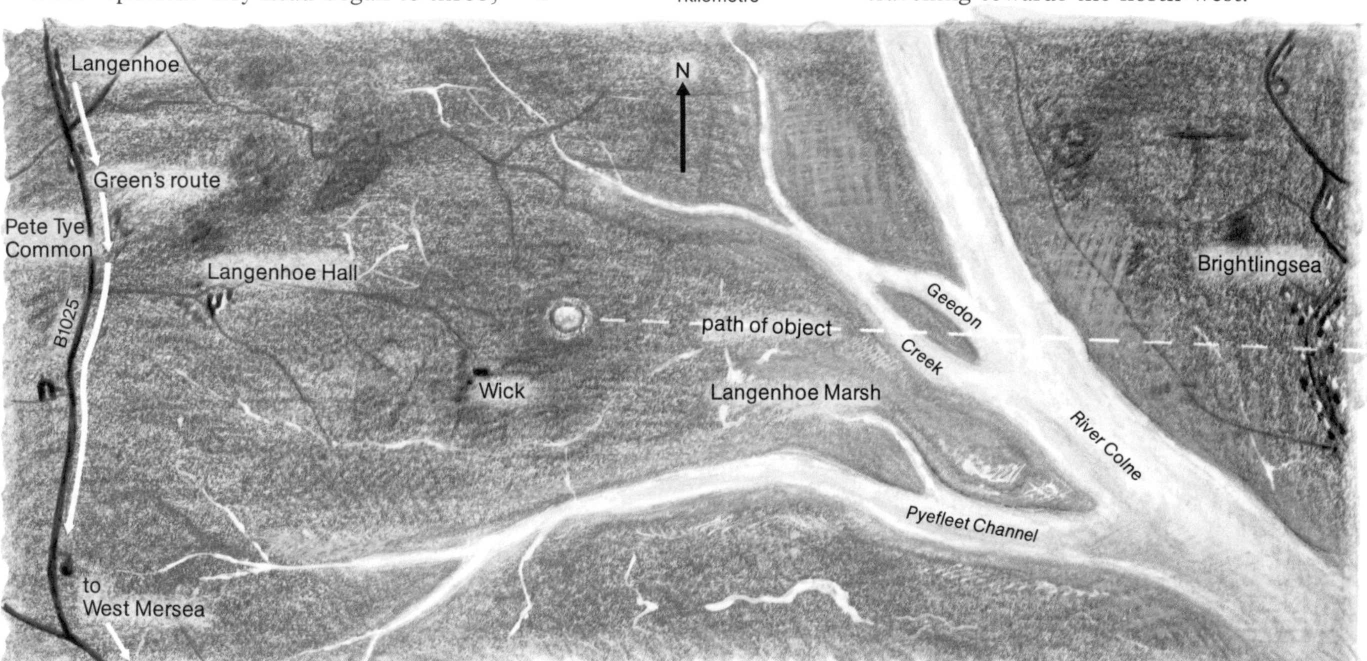

'A man in the flames'

Close encounter of the third kind: Felixstowe, Suffolk, England, 20 September 1965

Six days later, and about 20 miles (30 kilometres) from the scene of the Langenhoe close encounter of the second kind, a strange incident was reported. It may well have been a close encounter of the third kind.

Geoffrey Maskey, aged 25, had stopped his car in a Felixstowe lane known as Walton Avenue. With him were two friends, Michael Johnson and Mavis Fordyce. It was 10.30 p.m. when, without saying a word, Michael suddenly opened his door, got out and disappeared into the night. The others had been waiting for him for a few minutes when they heard a high-pitched humming noise.

Mavis was alarmed, and Geoff looked out of the car window to try to spot the source of the noise; he saw an orange-coloured, oval-shaped object some 6 feet (2 metres) in length, and about 100 feet (30 metres) above the lane. The orange glow lit up everything nearby.

The object then disappeared behind trees, with the humming noise still very much in evidence. Geoff called Michael's name and, when there was no response, reversed along the lane and called again. Suddenly Michael came stumbling through a hedge clutching his neck and his eyes; he staggered away from the car. The others thought he was having a game with them until he collapsed in the road. Geoff went over to him and found he was unconscious. They got him into the car and took him to Felixstowe Hospital.

Michael regained consciousness at the hospital, but did not recognise his companions. The doctor who examined him diagnosed severe shock. There were burn marks on the back of his neck, and a bump below his right ear. As a precaution Michael was transferred to Ipswich Hospital, and Geoff Maskey was not allowed to see him again until he was discharged next afternoon. Michael spoke then about a force that seemed to pull him from the car, and of 'a man in the flames pointing at him.'

The remarkable thing about this incident was that if indeed there had been 'a force' capable of pulling a man from a car (or, more likely, a mental compulsion, or enticement, to leave the car) then it was remarkably selective; neither Mavis nor Geoff felt its influence in any way.

This incident merited a brief news report in the *Ipswich Evening Star* of 21 September 1965. According to that newspaper the Felixstowe Hospital doctors spoke jocularly of 'Martians' and seemed – not surprisingly – to consider that the explanation given by Mr Maskey and Miss Fordyce was a tall story. It was suggested they had mistaken the flame from the local Propane Gas Plant flare-stack for a UFO. This the witnesses denied with vehemence.

Bearing in mind the Langenhoe sighting, it seems likely that there *was* something strange in the Felixstowe lane. But what?

UFO Photo File

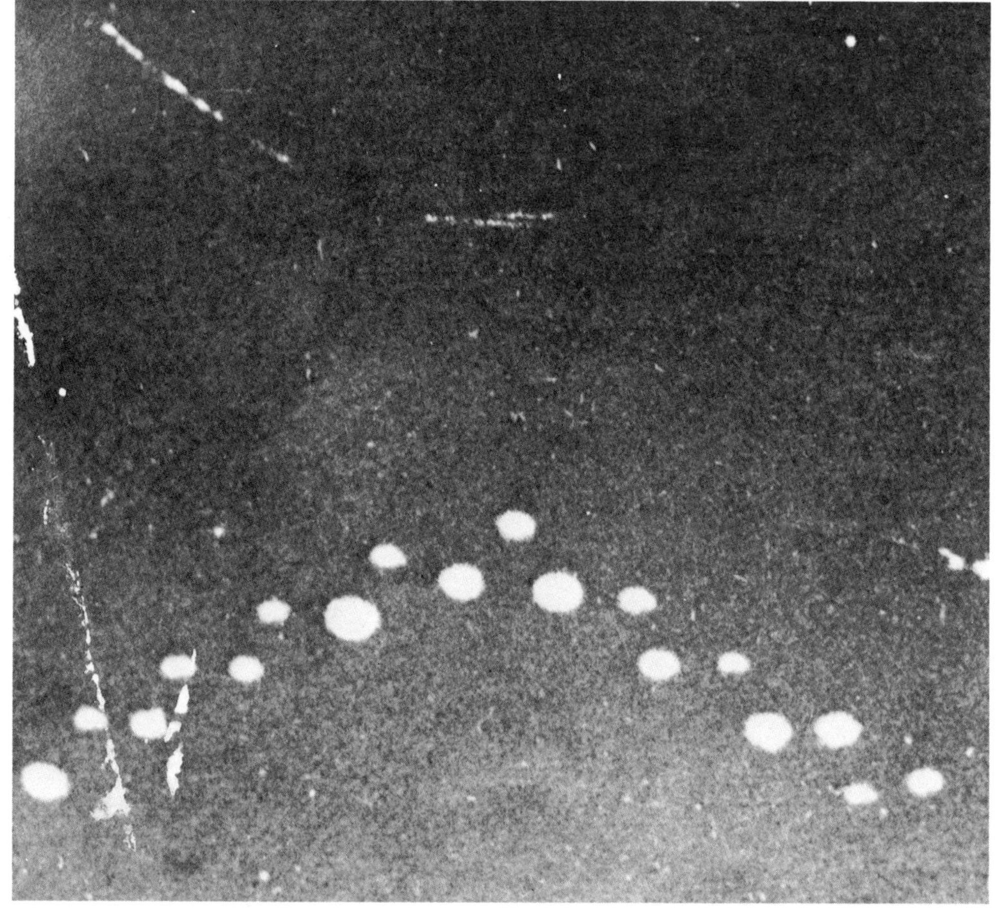

Above: this impressive photograph was taken during the Gemini XII space mission on 12 November 1966. Analysis has shown that the UFO that appears on the right of the picture is a distant object – but the NASA Photo Evaluation Lab claims this is actually rubbish that has been discarded from the Gemini XII spacecraft itself.

Left: at about 9.10 p.m. on 25 August 1951 a group of five professors and a postgraduate student were relaxing outside the house of Professor W.I. Robinson in Lubbock, Texas. Suddenly they saw a formation of bright lights flying rapidly across the sky. The professors estimated their speed at around 1800 miles per hour (2900 km/h) at a height of about one mile (1.5 kilometres). Sceptics claim that the lights were nothing more than reflections from the bellies of flying ducks – but if so, they would have been flying at more than 125 miles per hour (200 km/h) – which is far too fast for ducks!

The fishermen's tale

THE PASCAGOULA close encounter is one of the classics of UFO literature – deservedly so, if the story told by the witnesses is true. But is it? The case is typical of many UFO reports: there are few witnesses – in this case, the bulk of the information comes from one man, as the second witness lost consciousness at the beginning of the incident – and no reliable corroborative evidence. In such circumstances, even when sophisticated techniques such as lie detector tests and regressive hypnosis are used, only the personal integrity of the witnesses can guarantee their story.

'A very terrifying experience'

Close encounter of the third kind: Pascagoula, Mississippi, USA, 11 October 1973

The six-month period from October 1973 to March 1974 was a remarkable one for UFO reports. It was, in fact, one of the major 'flaps' and it visited, in particular, the United States, north-west Europe, Italy and Spain. One of the outstanding reports of that period in the USA came from Pascagoula, county town of Jackson County in the state of Mississippi. This town, whose population is just under 30,000, is situated at the south of the Pascagoula River on the coast of the Gulf of Mexico, about 100 miles (160 kilometres) to the east of New Orleans.

There were two witnesses, both of whom worked locally at the Walker Shipyard, Charles E. Hickson (45), a foreman, and Calvin R. Parker Jr (18), who allege that, on 11 October 1973, they experienced a close encounter with a UFO and its occupants, and abduction, while fishing from the pier of the Shaupeter shipyard on the Pascagoula River.

The time was about 9 p.m. when Hickson turned to get fresh bait. He says it was then that he heard a 'zipping' noise. Looking up, he saw an elongated, oval, bluish-grey craft – in a later interview he was to refer to it as 'a spacecraft' – which had very bright, flashing, 'blue-looking' lights. This object was hovering some 2 feet (60 centimetres) off the ground, and when the next move came the witness was a trifle puzzled, for he said: 'It seemed to open up, but really there wasn't a door there at all . . . and three creatures came *floating out* towards us. I was so scared I couldn't believe it was happening.'

The creatures were said to be pale, 'ghost-like', and about 5 feet (1.5 metres) tall. Their skin seemed to be wrinkled, and was a greyish colour, while in place of hands they had 'crab-like claws' or pincers. According to the witness's first report, these entities may have had slits for eyes, but he did not see them. They did have two small cone-shaped ears and a small pointed nose, with a hole below in the place of a mouth. They approached the two flabbergasted fishermen, floating just off the ground without moving their legs. A buzzing noise was heard from

one of them and, said Hickson, 'they were on us before we knew it.' The older man was paralysed with fear, and Parker passed out when, apparently, he was touched by one of the creatures.

Meanwhile two of the entities lifted Charlie Hickson from the ground, and they glided motionless into the craft. Hickson claims he had lost all sensation of feeling and weight. He was taken into a very brightly lit room – which, however, had no visible light fixtures. His friend was apparently taken into another room by the third entity. Hickson says he was placed in a reclining position and suspended in such a way that he did not touch any part of the craft. His limbs were completely paralysed; only his eyes were free to move. An instrument that looked like a big eye floated freely backwards and forwards about 9 inches (25 centimetres) above his body, and the creatures turned him so that all parts of his body came under the instrument's scrutiny. After some time Hickson was guided back outside the craft and was 'floated', together with Parker, back to his position on the pier, landing upright on his feet. He says he was so weak-kneed that he fell over.

Calvin Parker was unconscious throughout the incident, so all the evidence comes from Charlie Hickson. In his first interview, he said the UFO was about 10 feet (3 metres) wide, and something like 8 feet (2.5 metres) high. When it left, he said, it was gone from sight in less than a second. The occupants were like robots; they 'acted like they had a specific thing to do, and they did it. They didn't try to communicate with us. . . . I know now that they didn't intend to hurt us physically, but I feared they were going to take us away. I would like to emphasise that they didn't mean us any harm.'

That statement was made in an interview with the *Mississippi Press* a week after the incident. On the day of the encounter, Hickson and Parker had called at the *Press*'s offices, and found them closed; they then went to the sheriff's office, at 11 p.m., to make a report. Richard W. Heiden gave

Calvin Parker, who was 19 years old at the time of the close encounter at Pascagoula. He apparently fainted when one of the humanoids touched him, and remained unconscious throughout the incident. It was reported that he later suffered a nervous breakdown

details of what took place in a report to *Flying Saucer Review*. Sheriff Fred Diamond and Captain Glen Ryder interrogated the witnesses, doing everything they knew to break the stories, but to no avail. Ryder commented, 'If they were lying to me they should be in Hollywood.' The interviews were taped. Then the two officers left the witnesses alone and unaware that the recorder was still running. They spoke agitatedly about their experience, and Calvin Parker was so emotionally overcome that he started praying when Hickson left the room. The sheriff was convinced the two fishermen were telling the truth.

Next morning, Friday 12 October, detective Tom Huntley from the sheriff's office drove Hickson and Parker to Keesler Air Force Base at Biloxi, Mississippi, where they were checked for radiation. There was no evidence of contamination. While there they gave details of their experience to the head of intelligence at the base, who 'acted as though he'd heard it all before!'

On Sunday, 14 October, the witnesses were interviewed in Pascagoula by Dr J. Allen Hynek of Northwestern University, Evanston, Illinois, former civil scientific consultant on UFO reports to the US Air Force and a Consultant Editor to *The Unexplained*, and Dr James Harder of the University of California, Berkeley. Dr Harder hypnotised the men individually, regressing them to the time of the experience. They each relived the terror of the occasion to such an extent that Dr Harder said: 'The experience they underwent was indeed a real one. A very strong feeling of terror is practically impossible to fake under hypnosis.' Dr Hynek was more reserved: 'There is no question in my mind that these men have had a very terrifying experience.'

On 30 October, Hickson – but not Parker, who was apparently undergoing a nervous breakdown – underwent a polygraph examination (lie detector test) at the Pendleton Detective Agency in New Orleans. It was reported that the polygraph operator, one

Charlie Hickson, the principal witness, at the scene of the Pascagoula incident. Doubt is cast upon his reliability by the fact that details of his story varied substantially with each retelling

Above: Dr James Harder (left) and Dr J. Allen Hynek – a Consultant Editor to *The Unexplained* – interviewing Charlie Hickson and Calvin Parker shortly after their alleged abduction. Dr Harder hypnotically regressed the men to the time of their experience, and both scientists later agreed that the witnesses had had some very terrifying experience – although they were unable to say what it might have been

Scott Glasgow, was forced to admit after $2\frac{1}{2}$ hours of exhaustive tests that Hickson was telling the truth.

If this is true, it was a very strange remark for a polygraph operator to make. Polygraph tests are not sufficient to establish that a subject is lying; and any polygraph operator would have been well aware of this. In his book *UFOs explained*, Philip J. Klass claims that his own investigations have shown that Scott Glasgow was not, in fact, qualified as a polygraph operator. So it seems that, in spite of the newspaper publicity given to the fact that Hickson's story stood up to the lie detector test, it must remain inconclusive.

Hickson's experiences brought him considerable publicity; he appeared on television shows and even wrote a book. But unfortunately, his story often changed in the telling. Originally, for instance, he claimed that the UFO was some 10 feet (3 metres) long; in subsequent interviews, he said it was 20 or 30 feet (7 or 10 metres) long – quite a difference.

Hickson's descriptions of the alien creatures also varied on different occasions. In his original account, Hickson claimed they had two small cone-like ears, possibly slits where the eyes should have been, and a small sharp nose with a hole below it. Later, again on a television show, he said there were no eyes and that the hole below the nose was a slit. And more than a month after the incident, he disclosed for the first time that the light inside the spacecraft had been so bright that he had suffered severe eye injury, which had persisted for about three days.

These discrepancies, of course, tend to cast doubt upon the entire story – although they do not disprove it. But there are reports that possibly corroborate the evidence. Although no one but Hickson and Parker saw the UFO – despite the fact that the incident happened close to Highway 90, a busy road – many owners of television sets in the Pascagoula area reported interference.

On the same day, 11 October, 450 miles (700 kilometres) away near Hartwell, Georgia, a former Methodist minister was driving along when he saw a UFO land on the road in front of him. He also saw silver-suited, white-haired occupants.

On the same night, Police Chief Greenhaw of Falkville, Alabama, was telephoned by a woman who claimed that a 'spaceship' had landed in a field near her house. He raced to the location, armed with a Polaroid camera. There was nothing at the alleged site, but Greenhaw said he was confronted by a silver-suited creature on a side road. He took four Polaroid shots – which show a creature seemingly dressed in aluminium foil obligingly turned to face the camera. The entity apparently bolted, and Greenhaw gave chase in his patrol car, but failed to catch up with it – an inconclusive end to what seems to be a tall story.

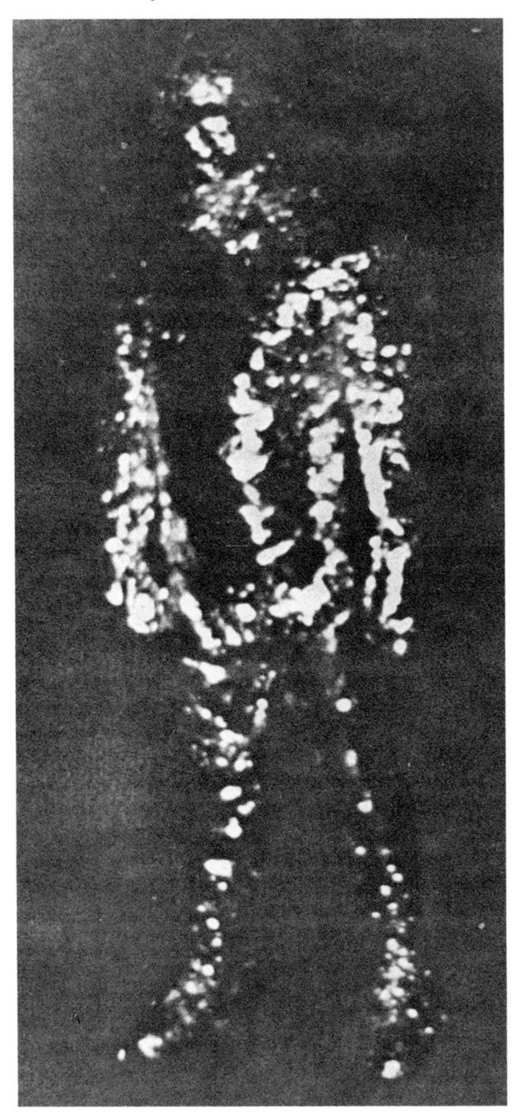

Right: a 'UFO entity' photographed with a Polaroid camera by Police Chief Jeff Greenhaw at Falkville, Alabama, on the night of the Pascagoula encounter. The entity reportedly bolted, and Greenhaw drove after it in his patrol car – but did not succeed in catching it

UFO Photo File

1

2

On the evening of 5 March 1979 Antonio Gonzales Llopis, aged 26, was taking photographs of the island of Gran Canaria in the Canary Islands when suddenly he noticed a strange, swirling light in the sky over the sea. A moment later a huge, dark object hurtled out of the sea straight up into the sky, surmounting a ball of fire (1, 2 and 3). Llopis pointed his camera at the object, checked its setting and continued to take pictures throughout the sighting, which he estimated lasted about three minutes – later verified by several other witnesses.

The brilliant light surrounding the dark object effectively obscured any detail, but it seemed to accelerate rapidly, shooting 'through' the pattern of lights in the sky. After the object had disappeared a bright trail and a golden cloud illuminated the sky for half an hour (4 and 5). Thousands of people on Gran Canaria reported the incident and many of them took photographs. Some of these found their way into the files of the Spanish government, which is, however, increasingly sympathetic to serious UFO investigation.

3

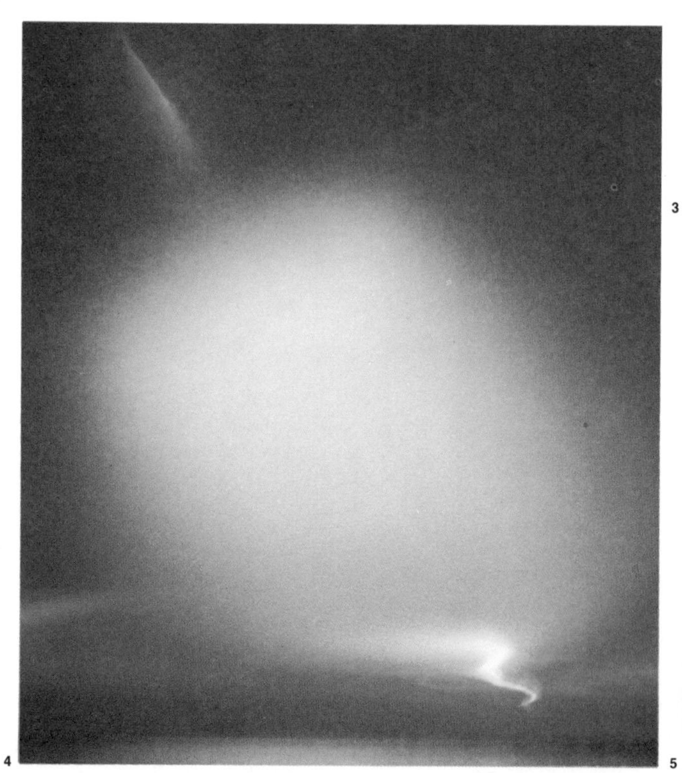
4

5

Right: bright lights seen near the major airport of Barajas, 6 miles (10 kilometres) from Madrid, Spain, one night in December 1979. An estimated 10 lights appeared suddenly over Madrid, executed a brief aerial ballet then sped off in the direction of Barajas, where this photograph was taken. UFOs seem to be fascinated with airports and aircraft, naval bases and ships, nuclear power stations and military establishments of all kinds. Believers in the extra-terrestrial hypothesis claim that the UFOs are aliens showing an interest in the hardware of our technology to compare our progress with theirs. More down-to-earth observers suggest that UFOs are in fact secret weapons accidentally seen while undergoing trials in the vicinity of the military bases from which they came.

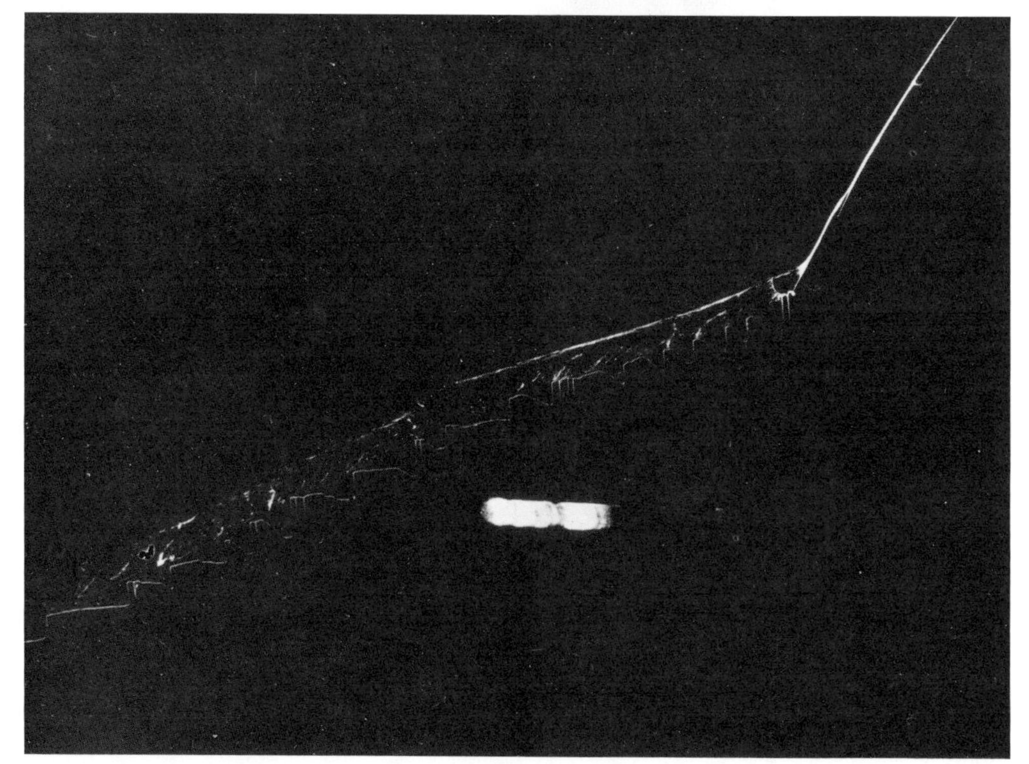

Left: photograph of a UFO seen near Lakeville, Connecticut, USA, on the night of 23 January 1967, and taken by a 17-year-old pupil from a local boys' boarding school. This was only one of the many sightings of 'bright lights moving erratically' reported over a four-month period, mainly by boys from the school, although one teacher and a 12-year-old boy who lived nearby added their testimony. Condon Report officers Ayer and Wadsworth investigated and studied the student's picture. The boy described the UFO as 'a bright point of light that blinked or pulsated regularly'. He said it 'pulsated twice' then disappeared behind Indian Mountain. The investigators left the case open – but could the UFOs have been secret weapons undergoing night trials? Or were they really 'nuts and bolts' alien spacecraft?

A logic of their own

ONE OF THE MOST curious categories in the UFO files consists of isolated reports of UFOs landing on rivers or lakes and siphoning up considerable quantities of water. We report on two cases, widely separated in both space and time: the first is from Japan in 1973, the second from northern Italy in 1952. In both instances, the amount of water taken on board by the UFOs suggests that it is not intended merely for scientific analysis – yet what else can it be used for? Are we to believe that UFOs are powered or cooled by water, or that their occupants need water for drinking or cooking?

Our third case is one of the weirdest ever to have been reported in Japan. Although it must be classified as a close encounter of the third kind, no UFO was observed during the incident. If some alien entities can survive without spacecraft, why are others so apparently vulnerable that they require regular supplies of water? The reports simply do not add up to a coherent picture of the perplexing UFO phenomenon.

'Infinite menace'

Close encounter of the third kind: Tomakomai, Hokkaido, Japan, July 1973

In 1975 *Flying Saucer Review* received an exciting account of one of the occasional sightings of UFOs taking on water. It came from a Japanese UFO investigator, Jun-Ichi Takanashi of Osaka; shadowy humanoid beings were also said to have been observed. The event took place at Tomakomai, a small industrial town on the southern coast of Hokkaido, the northernmost island of Japan, in July 1973. The eyewitness was Masaaki Kudou, a university student, then aged 20. He was home on vacation, and had taken a temporary job as a night security guard at a timber yard.

After patrolling the premises in his car, Mr Kudou returned to the prescribed place from which he could observe the premises – and the waters of the bay beyond – and settled back to listen to his radio, light a cigarette, and relax. It was a still night, with the stars clearly visible. Suddenly he saw a streak of light flash across the sky, a spectacular 'shooting star' that suddenly stopped in its tracks, vanished, and reappeared. Remaining stationary, the light now expanded and contracted alternately at high speed, growing until it reached the apparent size of a baseball held at arm's length. It darted about in all directions within a few degrees of arc, and Mr Kudou found himself dizzily trying to follow its gyrations. As it began to descend spirally towards the sea the young student felt a surge of alarm, especially when the light halted near a distant cement works, and began to direct a beam of intermittent pulses of green light towards the north. Next, the object continued its descent towards the sea, this time sweeping in an arc until it was in a position much closer to the student observer. It halted its descent at about 70 feet (20 metres) from the sea, and the student saw a transparent tube emerge and lower itself towards the water. A soft *min-min-min-min* noise could be heard as this was happening, and the pitch of the noise lowered as the tube descended. When the tube touched the water its lower edge glowed, and it seemed that water was being sucked up into the object above.

Masaaki Kudou wondered if he were dreaming or, failing that, if his imagination were playing tricks with him. He lowered his gaze for a minute or so; when he looked again the water-suction operation was over, and the tube had been withdrawn from the water. No sooner had he registered this fact than the hovering UFO began to move towards him with what seemed to be infinite menace; he feared he was about to be attacked, and probably killed.

The object moved into a position some 160 feet (50 metres) above Kudou's car, and he, by leaning forwards and looking up, could keep it in view. He says its surface was as smooth as a table-tennis ball and, emitting its own glow, appeared to be white. Around his car everything was lit up as though by daylight, and he says he saw what appeared to be windows around the diameter of the spherical object. In the middle of one of these there was a shadowy human-shaped figure, while to the right there were two smaller shapes in another of the windows, but Kudou could not see whether or not these were similar to the first. All this, plus a sudden feeling that he was bound hand and foot, was too much for the witness, who rocked his head in his hands, with his chin on the steering wheel, moaning to himself.

Nevertheless, he still felt an urge to look upwards and, straining to do this, Kudou saw in the sky above the car three or four newly arrived glowing objects, similar in all respects to the first one. There was also a large, dark brown object, in silhouette, which looked like 'three gasoline drums connected together lengthwise' and which hovered noiselessly.

Suddenly the whole phenomenal spectacle came to an end. The glowing spheres swiftly manoeuvred into position whence they disappeared into one end of the large 'gasoline can' objects, and this in turn shot off to the north rather like a shooting star. The witness sat motionless, numb all over. He slowly became aware that his car radio was giving forth meaningless sounds, and that he himself was suffering from a severe headache. He was later able to estimate that the terrifying incident had lasted for about 12 minutes in all.

'They want to do me harm'

Close encounter of the third kind: Lucca, Italy, 25 July 1952

At 3 a.m. on 25 July 1952, a keen fisherman named Carlo Rossi was walking alongside the River Serchio, opposite San Pietro a Vico in Lucca, northern Italy, when he was puzzled by the appearance of an unusual light from an unseen position on the river below. Climbing the high embankment, he looked down to see a huge circular craft bearing a transparent cupola on top, and a shallow turret underneath from which three legs protruded, supporting the body of the craft above the water. There was also a ladder, and a long tube by which, apparently, the craft was taking in water. Suddenly a port opened in the upper part of the turret, and Carlo saw a 'human' figure look out. This figure pointed at the fisherman, who scrambled down the embankment. A green ray passed over his head, and he threw himself down. Looking up, seconds later, he saw the craft rise above the embankment and move off at high speed towards Viareggio.

Rossi was badly shaken by the incident – but something that happened a few weeks later worried him much more. To the outsider, the incident seems trivial – although it is a classic example of an MIB encounter: a strange man approached Rossi and offered him, Rossi said, a 'bad' cigarette. Rossi was terrified; he used later to say, 'I wonder if they want to do me harm, maybe, because of the thing I saw in the river?'

The circumstances of Rossi's subsequent death seem to lend substance to his suspicion. He was riding home on his bicycle one day when he was knocked down by a car. The driver was never identified.

'Alarm turned to terror'

Close encounter of the third kind: Sayama City, Saitama Prefecture, Japan, 3 October 1978

Right: Mr Hideichi Amano, victim of the Sayama encounter, recounts his experience on the television programme *11 P.M.*

Mr Hideichi Amano, who owns and runs a snack bar in Sayama City, Saitama Prefecture, Japan, is also a keen radio 'ham'. Jun-Ichi Takanashi investigated Mr Amano's alarming experience after seeing him on the television programme *11 P.M.*

The encounter occurred on the evening of 3 October 1978, when Amano, using his mobile unit radio car, drove up a mountain outside Sayama City at about 8.30 p.m. with his two-year-old daughter Juri. He made the trip so that he could get unrestricted radio transmission and reception for a conversation with his brother, who lives in a distant part of the country. When their hook-up was finished, and a few other local calls had been made, Hideichi Amano was about to drive back down the mountain when the interior of the car became very bright, a light ten times brighter than was normal was coming from the fluorescent tube he had fitted inside the car. He observed that this light was confined to the car's interior; none, he said, was passing through the windows! Moments earlier Juri had been standing on the passenger seat beside him, but now her father was aghast to see the child lying on the seat, and foaming at the mouth. At the same instant he became aware of a round patch of orange light that was beamed through the windscreen and onto his stomach, and he saw that this was coming from a point in the sky. And then alarm turned to terror when he sensed something metallic being pressed against his right temple.

Hideichi Amano glanced sideways and saw an unearthly humanoid creature standing there with a pipe-like device in its mouth, and it was this that was being pressed against his head. From the tube came an incessant babble, as from a tape being played too fast.

The witness said the creature had a round face, but no neck, two sharply pointed ears, two small, motionless eyes that glowed bluish-white, and a triangular depression on its forehead. The mouth was clamped round the pipe, and no nose could be seen. While the babble continued Mr Amano says he found it difficult to move, and his mind became 'vague'. The terrified radio ham tried to start the car to flee the place, but there was no response from the engine, and the lights would not work, either. Then, after four or five minutes, the creature began to dim out and slowly vanished. The orange light disappeared, the interior lighting returned to normal, and other equipment that had been switched on now began to function. When the headlights returned Mr Amano switched the starter and got an instant response. Still in a confused state he roared away down the hill, and it was only when he reached the lower slopes that he remembered little Juri's condition. He stopped and, fortunately, the child stood up and said: 'I want a drink of water, papa.'

The witness decided to report the experience to the police, but they only poked fun at him, so he went home and retired to bed, still suffering a severe headache.

Researchers for the *11 P.M.* programme heard of the affair and eventually arranged for Mr Amano to be questioned under hypnosis in front of the cameras. One piece of information retrieved was that the creature was alleged to have told him to return to the meeting place at a certain time – which, to avoid a stampede by the curious, was not revealed to the viewers. Jun-Ichi Takanashi seemed to have little faith in the regression session because the 'hypnotist's insistence on more information was far too severe'; he suspected that the idea of a second meeting with the humanoid was a creation of the witness's subconscious mind. The fact that no second meeting was ever reported seems to lend weight to this. Yet, despite his reservations, Takanashi considered the encounter, as originally reported, to be 'the strangest ever to have taken place in Japan.'

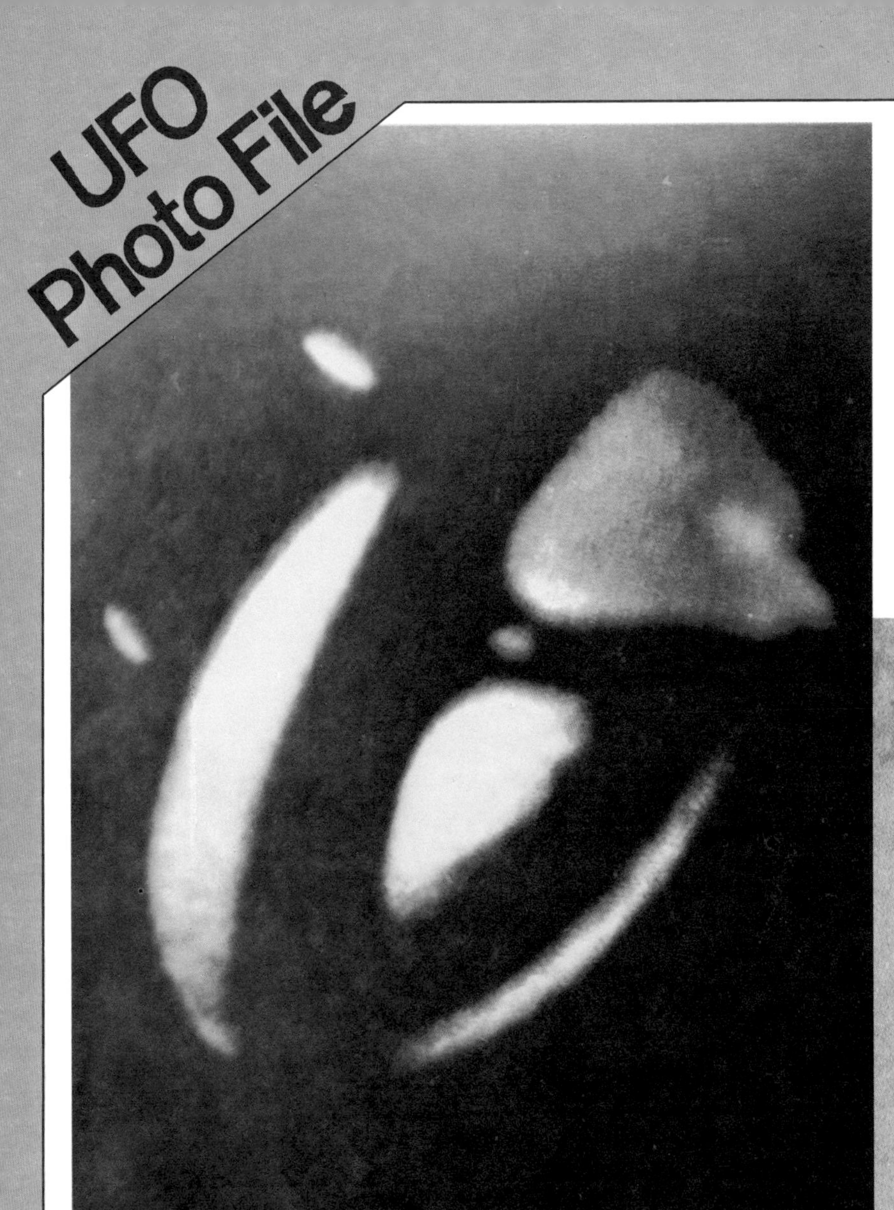

Left: this, one of the rare photographs of a nocturnal UFO to show more than an indeterminate blur of light, was taken by a 14-year-old paper-boy in Tulsa, Oklahoma, USA, on 2 August 1965. The object was observed by many witnesses, who stated that the tricoloured lights changed slowly to a uniform blue-green. The Condon Committee confirmed that the photograph represented a large object seen against a background of sky – and that the dark stripes between the bright patches were neither space nor sky, but some kind of structure, part of the UFO itself. With characteristic caution, the US Air Force concluded that the photograph represented either a genuine UFO – or a tricoloured Christmas tree light! The UFO organisation Ground Saucer Watch, on the other hand, considers it strong UFO evidence.

Right: at about 9.00 a.m. one day in September 1957 this strange, ring-shaped object was seen in the sky over Fort Belvoir, Virginia, USA. It 'seemed solid', very black with no reflection. It seemed to be about 60 feet (18 metres) in diameter. The ring gradually became engulfed in black smoke and finally disappeared. The Condon Committee identified the sighting as 'an atomic bomb simulation demonstration of the type commonly carried out at Fort Belvoir at this period'.

Left: a still from a film taken by Ralph Mayher in Miami, Florida, USA, on 29 July 1952. Using computer techniques to analyse the photograph, the UFO organisation Ground Saucer Watch has established that it is probably genuine and that it shows an object 30 to 40 feet (9 to 12 metres) long. Mr Mayher reported that its speed appeared to be less than that of a falling meteorite as it shot away over the ocean.

Puzzled by his sighting, Mr Mayher turned his film over to the US Air Force for investigation. It was never returned to him. Many people see the incident as part of a deliberate campaign on the part of the US authorities to suppress evidence for the existence of UFOs. Luckily, Mr Mayher had foreseen the possibility of his film getting 'lost': before handing it over to the USAF, he carefully snipped off the first few frames. This is one of them.

The closest encounter ever

ONE OF THE EARLIEST reports of an alleged abduction by humanoids was kept secret for over three years because it was deemed too 'wild' by those who first interviewed the abductee. And in the early reports the witness was known only as 'A.V.B.' to preserve his anonymity.

This amazing case first became known when the victim wrote to João Martins, a Brazilian journalist, and his medical friend Dr Olavo T. Fontes towards the end of 1957. Apparently, the man with the strange story was a young farmer who lived near the small town of São Francisco de Sales in Minas Gerais, Brazil. Intrigued, Martins and Fontes sent the farmer financial aid to make the long journey to Rio de Janeiro, where the investigation began on 22 February 1958 in Dr Fontes's consulting room.

The story that unfolded was, the investigators felt, so astonishing that they decided to 'keep it on ice' in case a similar incident occurred that might corroborate any of the details. And they feared that if the account became widely known there would be a rash of 'copycat' cases, which would end up invalidating this story. But a few details did leak out – fortunately in the right direction, for the outline of the tale reached the ears of Dr Walter Buhler in 1961, and he began to make his own detailed investigation.

The Buhler report eventually appeared as a newsletter and this, translated by Gordon Creighton and supplemented with editorial comments, appeared in *Flying Saucer Review* in January 1965. Very soon after, João Martin's account was published in the Spanish language edition – not the Portuguese as might have been expected – of the Brazilian magazine *O Cruzeiro*. Finally the full case, including the results of various detailed clinical reports, was included in *The humanoids*, a collection of accounts of encounters with UFO occupants, in 1969. At last the story that had been thought too 'wild' to be made known to the public was in print, and 'A.V.B.' was revealed to be 23-year-old Antônio Villas Boas.

'I am going to bear our child'

Close encounter of the third kind: São Francisco de Sales, Brazil, 15 October 1957

Antônio Villas Boas: his remarkable experience was at first concealed by UFO researchers because they considered it too wild

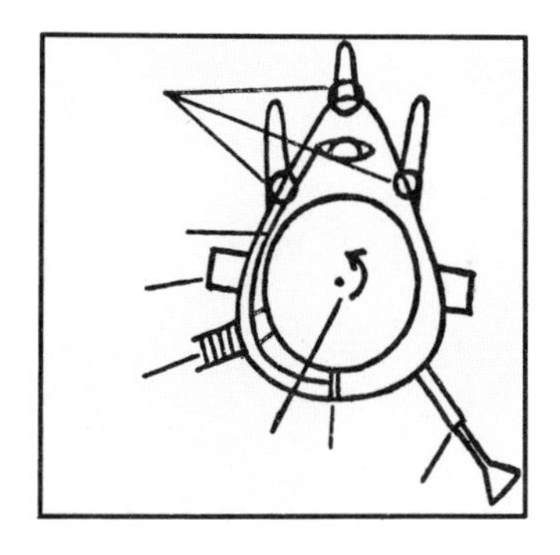

These sketches of the UFO were made by Villas Boas in February 1958 (above) for Dr Olavo Fontes, and in July 1961 (below) for Drs Buhler and Aquino of the Brazilian Society for the Study of Flying Saucers

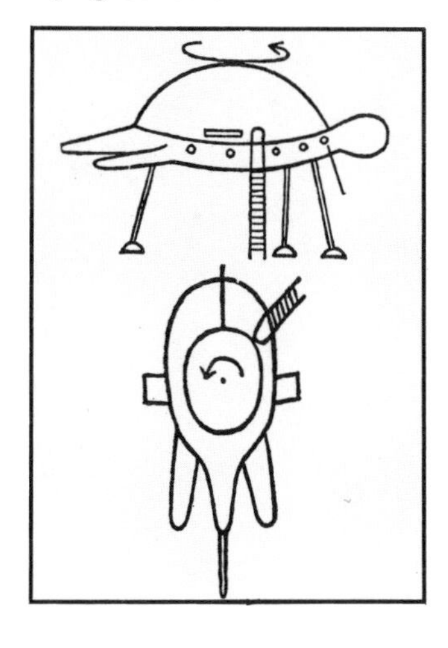

The actual abduction of Antônio Villas Boas was heralded by two unusual events. The first took place on 5 October 1957 when he and his brother were retiring to bed at about 11 p.m. after a party. From their bedroom window they saw an unidentified light in the farmyard below. It moved up onto the roof of their house, and together they watched it shine through the slats of the shutters and the gaps in the tiles (there being no ceiling proper) before it departed.

The second strange incident occurred on 14 October at about 9.30 p.m. when the Villas Boas brothers were out ploughing with their tractor. They suddenly saw a dazzling light, 'big and round', about 100 yards (90 metres) above one end of the field. Antônio went over for a closer look, but – as if playing games with him – the light moved swiftly to the other end of the field, a manoeuvre it repeated the two or three times the young farmer tried to get a closer look at it. Then the light abruptly vanished.

The following night, 15 October, Antônio was out in the field again, ploughing alone by the light of his headlamps. Suddenly, at about 1 a.m., he became aware of a 'large red star' that seemed to be descending towards the end of the field. As it came nearer he saw that it was in fact a luminous egg-shaped object. The UFO's approach brought it right overhead, about 50 yards (45 metres) above the tractor. The whole field became as bright as if it were broad daylight.

Villas Boas sat in his cab transfixed with fear as the object landed about 15 yards (15 metres) in front of him. He saw a rounded object with a distinct rim that was apparently clustered with purple lights. A huge round headlamp on the side facing him seemed to be producing the 'daylight' effect. There was a revolving cupola on top, and as he watched, fascinated, he saw three shafts – or 'legs' – emerge and reach for the ground. At this the terrified farmer started to drive off but after a short distance the engine stopped, despite the fact that it had been running smoothly. Villas Boas found he count not restart it and in a panic he leapt from the cab and set off across the heavily ploughed field. The deep ruts proved a handicap to his escape and he had gone only a few paces when someone grabbed his arm. As he turned, he was astonished to see a strangely garbed individual whose helmeted head reached only to Villas Boas's shoulder. He hit out at his assailant, who was knocked flying, but he was quickly grabbed by three other humanoids who lifted him from the ground as he struggled and shouted. He later said:

> I noticed that as they were dragging me towards the machine my speech seemed to arouse their surprise or curiosity, for they stopped and peered attentively at my face as I spoke, though without loosening their grip on me. This relieved me a little as to their intentions, but I still did not stop struggling. . . .

He was carried to the craft. A ladder descended from a door, and his captors hoisted him up this with great difficulty – especially as he tried to resist by hanging on to a kind of handrail. But in the end they succeeded.

Once inside the machine Villas Boas found himself in a square room with metallic walls, brightly lit by small, high lamps. He was set down on his feet, and became aware that there were five small beings, two of whom held him firmly. One signalled that he should be taken through to an adjoining room, which was larger, and oval in shape, with a metal column that reached from floor to ceiling, together with a table and some swivel chairs set to one side.

A 'conversation' ensued between his captors, who made sounds like dog barks:

> Those sounds were so totally different from anything I had heard until now. They were slow barks and yelps, neither very clear nor very hoarse, some longer, some shorter, at times containing several different sounds all at once, and at other times ending in a quaver. But they were simply sounds, animal barks, and nothing could be distinguished that could be taken as the sound of a syllable or word of a foreign language. Not a thing! To me it sounded alike, so that I am unable to retain a word of it . . . I still shudder when I think of those sounds. I can't reproduce them . . . my voice just isn't made for that.

Handled by humanoids

This strange communication ceased abruptly, when all five set about him, stripping him of his clothing while he shouted and struggled – but to no avail. (Apparently they stopped to peer at him whenever he yelled, and, strangely, although they seemed to be using force, at no time did they hurt him.)

The beings were all dressed in tight-fitting grey overalls and large, broad helmets reinforced with bands of metal at back and front. There were apertures through which Villas Boas could see light-coloured eyes. Three tubes emerged from the top of each helmet, the central one running down the back and entering the clothing in line with the spine; the other two curved away to enter the clothes, one beneath each armpit. The sleeves ended in thick gloves, which seemed difficult to bend at the fingers. The trouser part fitted closely over seat, thighs and lower legs, and the footwear seemed an integral part of this section, the soles being very thick – perhaps as much as 2 inches (5 centimetres). On his chest each being had a kind of breastplate or 'shield' 'about the size of a slice of pineapple', which reflected light, and the shield was joined to a belt at the waist by a strip of laminated metal.

The naked and shivering farmer – it was a

Below: Villas Boas's impression of the inscription above a door in the humanoids' craft. In the statement he made to Dr Fontes, Villas Boas said it was 'a sort of luminous inscription – or something similar – traced out in red symbols which, owing to the effect of the light, seemed to stand out about 2 inches (5 centimetres) in front of the metal of the door. This inscription was the only thing of its kind that I saw in the machine. The signs were scrawls completely different from what we know as lettering'

chilly night outside, and no warmer in the craft – stood there quaking and 'worried to death'. He wondered what on earth was going to happen to him. One of the little creatures approached him with what seemed to be a sort of wet sponge, which he rubbed all over Villas Boas's skin. He said: 'The liquid was as clear as water, but quite thick, and without smell. I thought it was some sort of oil, but was wrong, for my skin did not become greasy or oily.'

He was now led to another door, which had an inscription in red over it. He tried to memorise this, although it meant nothing to him, being written in unknown characters. In yet another room one of the beings approached with a sort of chalice from which dangled two flexible tubes; one of these, with a capped end like a child's suction 'arrow', was fixed to his chin, while the other tube was pumped up and down. The alarmed Villas Boas watched the chalice fill with what was presumably his own blood. The creatures then left him alone. He sat on a soft couch contemplating the nightmarish situation in which he found himself.

Suddenly he smelt a strange odour, which made him feel sick. He examined the walls and saw metallic tubes at just below ceiling level. Grey smoke was coming through perforations in the tubes. Villas Boas rushed to a corner of the room and vomited, and after that he felt a little less frightened. Moments later there was a noise at the door, which opened to reveal a woman standing there. As Villas Boas gaped, the woman walked towards him. Flabbergasted, he realised she was as naked as he was.

The woman, said Villas Boas, was more beautiful than anyone he had met before. She was shorter than he, her head reaching only to his shoulder – he is 5 feet 5 inches (1.6 metres). Her hair was smooth, and very fair, almost white, and as though bleached. Parted in the centre, it reached halfway down her neck, with ends curling inwards. Her eyes were large, blue and elongated, 'slanted outwards'. Her small nose was straight, neither pointed nor turned up. She had high cheekbones, but – as Villas Boas discovered – they were soft and fleshy to the touch. Her face was wide, but narrowed to a markedly

pointed chin. Her lips were thin, the mouth being almost like a slit. The ears were normal, but small.

The door closed, and Villas Boas found himself alone with this woman, whose slim body was the most beautiful he had ever seen. She had high, well-separated breasts. Her waist was slender, her hips wide and her thighs large, while her feet were small and her hands long and narrow. He saw too that the hair in her armpits, and her pubic hair, was blood red. He smelt no perfume on her, 'apart from the feminine odour'.

She approached the farmer and rubbed her head against his (presumably by standing on tip-toe). Her body felt as though glued to his, and she made it quite clear what she wanted. His excitement welled up. The sexual act was normal – as was the one that followed – but then she tired, and refused further advances.

Villas Boas recalled that she never kissed him, but once gently bit him on his chin. Although she never spoke, she grunted, and that 'nearly spoiled everything, giving the disagreeable impression that I was with an animal'.

When she was called away by one of the other beings, she turned to Villas Boas, pointed to her belly, and then pointed to the sky. These gestures instilled a great fear in Antônio – a fear that was with him still, four years after the event – for he interpreted them as meaning she would return to take him away. Dr Fontes later calmed him by suggesting that she meant: 'I am going to bear our child, yours and mine, there on my home planet.' This led to speculation by the farmer that all they wanted was 'a good stallion' to improve their stock.

Then Villas Boas was told to get dressed, after which he says he was taken on a conducted tour round the craft; during this he tried to steal an instrument for a keepsake, only to be rebuffed, angrily, by one of the crew. Eventually, he was invited to go down the ladder, and back onto solid ground. From there he watched the ladder retract, while the metal legs and the lights began to glow. The craft rose into the air with its cupola turning at great speed. With lights flashing it listed slightly to one side, then suddenly shot off like a bullet.

It was by then 5.30 a.m. and the abductee's adventure had lasted over four hours.

He returned home hungry, and weakened by his spell of vomiting. He slept through to 4.30 p.m. and awoke feeling perfectly normal. But when he fell asleep again he slept badly, and woke up shouting after dreaming of the incident. Next day he was troubled by nausea and a violent headache. When that left him his eyes began to burn. Unusual wounds, with infections, appeared on parts of his body. When they dried up they left round, purplish scars.

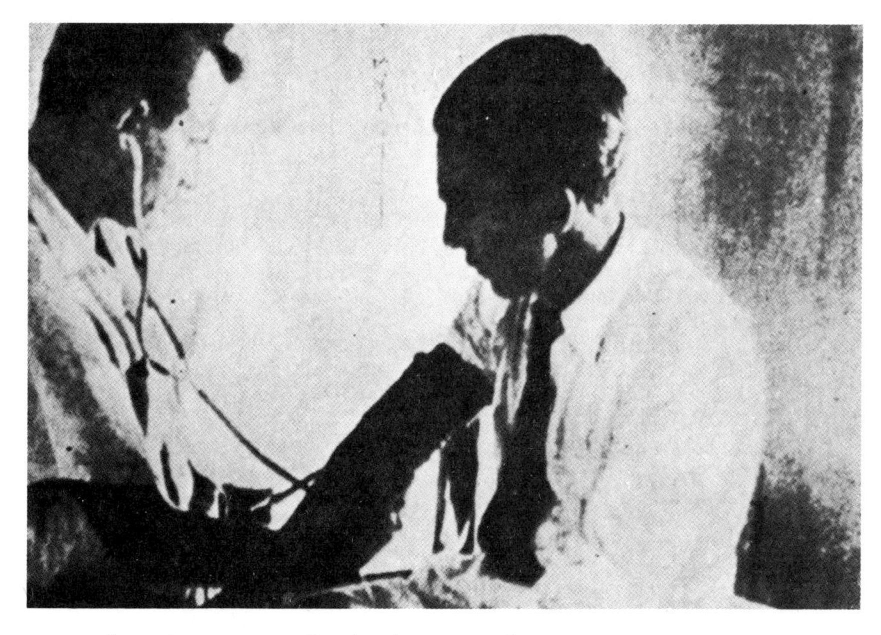

Villas Boas was examined by Dr Fontes in February 1958, four months after the alleged abduction. The symptoms he described suggested 'radiation poisoning or exposure to radiation', but it was too late for this diagnosis to be confirmed

Mysterious scars

When Dr Fontes examined Villas Boas, he observed two small patches, one on each side of the chin. He described these as 'scars of some superficial lesion with associated sub-cutaneous haemorrhage'. Several other mysterious scars on his body were also noted.

In a letter to *Flying Saucer Review* Dr Fontes suggested that the symptoms described pointed to radiation poisoning, or exposure to radiation. Wrote Dr Fontes: 'Unfortunately he came to me too late for the blood examinations that could have confirmed such a possibility beyond doubt.'

On 10 October 1971 João Martins was at last officially cleared to write about the case for the Brazilian public. His account appeared in the Rio de Janeiro Sunday review *Domingo Illustrado.* His abridged account concluded with a statement that:

> A.V.B. was subjected by us [Martins, Dr Fontes, and a *military officer* – whose presence was not revealed in the earlier reports] to the most sophisticated methods of interrogation, without falling into any contradictions. He resisted every trap we set to test whether he was seeking notoriety or money. A medical examination . . . revealed a state of completely normal physical and mental equilibrium. His reputation in the region where he lives was that of an honest, serious, hardworking man.

Martins also revealed that the interrogation at times bordered on harsh and cruel treatment, just short of physical violence, but Villas Boas never veered from his original story in any detail. The journalist concluded: 'If this story be true, it may well be that, somewhere out there in the Universe, there is a strange child . . . that maybe is being prepared to return here. Where does fantasy end? Where does reality begin?'

UFOs over water

AN INTERESTING subspecies of UFO reports describes cases in which the objects have emerged from or disappeared into water – most often the sea. One such famous, and well-documented, instance is the extraordinary series of photographs previously examined which were taken in the Canary Islands. Some writers have even suggested that there are enormous UFO 'bases' hidden under the world's oceans. In the absence of any concrete evidence, however, it seems best to leave this speculation where it belongs, in the realm of science fiction.

All the cases that follow occurred, intriguingly, within 200 miles (320 kilometres) of each other along the Brazilian coast south of Rio de Janeiro (see map), though they were all well-separated in time. All involved several witnesses and what appear to be indubitably 'nuts and bolts' craft. Only the Santos case seems amenable to a conventional explanation: but if it represents a stray rocket, aircraft pod, or satellite debris, why were the authorities unable to locate the wreckage at the site of the crash?

'A motor boat striking the water'

Close encounter of the third kind: Rio de Janeiro, Brazil, 27 June 1970

On Sunday, 27 June 1970 Senhor Aristeu Machado and his five daughters were playing a game on the verandah of their home, 318 Avenida Niemeyer, Rio de Janeiro, from which they could look out over the road below to the South Atlantic Ocean beyond. With them was their friend and neighbour Senhor João Aguiar, an official of the Brazilian Federal Police.

Dona Maria Nazaré, who was preparing lunch in the kitchen, called out to check the time: it was 11.38 a.m. About two minutes after that Senhor Aguiar happened to look out over the sea, and quickly drew the attention of the others to 'a motor boat striking the water'. As this object descended it threw up spray on all sides.

The game and lunch were quickly forgotten for, as the family and their guest watched the 'motor boat' they could see two 'bathers' aboard the craft, who seemed to be signalling with their arms. In a statement to Dr Walter Buhler, who investigated the case, Aguiar said there were definitely two persons on board and that they were wearing 'shining clothing, and something on their heads'. The craft was a greyish metallic colour; it seemed to be between 15 and 20 feet (5 and 6 metres) in length and had a transparent cupola. One strange feature was noted: at no time did the object make the 'bobbing' movement associated with a boat on a swell.

Above: the Avenida Niemeyer, which runs north-east along the coast into the suburbs of Leblon and Ipanema near Rio de Janeiro. The Machados' house stands above it to the left of the picture

Right: Senhor Aristeu Machado and his wife on the verandah from which they watched the UFO and subsequent events in the sea

Sr Aguiar ran down to the nearby Mar Hotel, and telephoned the Harbour Police; they promised to send help to the occupants of the 'motor boat', who were presumably involved in a mishap offshore. Aguiar then returned to the house and rejoined the Machados on their verandah. He had been away from the house for about 30 minutes.

Shortly after Aguiar returned, the object – which was now seen to be disc-shaped – took off; it had been on the surface for 40 to 45 minutes. It skimmed the water for some 300 yards (280 metres), throwing off a wave from the bows at it went, then lifted from the sea and made off quickly towards the south-east. It was then that the witnesses realised it was not a motor boat, but rather an object that looked like a *flying saucer*. A hexagonal-shaped appendage retracted into the underside of the main body, and a number of lights on the appendage flashed, in sequence, green, yellow, red.

Once airborne, the object appeared to be transparent rather than aluminium-coloured, and Dona Maria Nazaré said she clearly saw two entities sitting inside. There was little traffic noise from the road at that time, but the witnesses could hear no sound from the object.

On the sea where the UFO had originally rested, the witnesses saw a white hoop-shaped object 'about the size of a trunk or chest', according to Dona Maria Nazaré. Suddenly the hoop sank, then it reappeared and a yellow oval-shaped section separated from it. This, it was estimated, was some 16 inches (40 centimetres) across with about 8 inches (20 centimetres) projecting above the surface of the water. It remained stationary for about three minutes, then began to move towards the shore, with its longer axis directed at the witnesses. A green flange at the rear of the object separated from the main body and followed it at a distance of about a yard (1 metre). After 15 minutes the yellow oval was about 130 yards (120 metres) from the shore, when it made a right-angled turn to its left and headed for the beach at Gávea – a movement directly opposed to the maritime current in the area at the time.

The white hoop disappeared several times, but when it came back into view it was still pursuing its direct course for Gávea Beach, as though it were going to link up once again with the yellow object.

Meanwhile the police launch from Fort Copacabana had arrived at the spot where the UFO had remained stationary, having come into view about 20 minutes after João Aguiar made his telephone call. So it seems likely that the crew must have seen the UFO take off. At roughly the position where the hoop had been left the launch stopped and the police hauled on board a red cylindrical object. They then made off at speed towards their base.

No statement was made by the police regarding what they saw or found. And, although an account of the incident appeared in the newspaper *Diário de Notícias* on 28 June 1970, no other witnesses came forward to confirm the sighting.

'Like beads in a necklace'

Close encounter of the second kind: near Curitiba, Brazil, 10 January 1958

On 10 January 1958 Captain Chrysólogo Rocha was sitting with his wife in the porch of a house overlooking the sea near Curitiba, and was surprised to see an unfamiliar 'island'. He had his binoculars with him, and when he had focused on the island he was amazed to see that it was growing in size. He cried out to people inside the house, and very soon eight of them joined the couple on the porch to witness the strange phenomenon.

The object seemed to consist of two parts, one in the sea and the other suspended above it. Then, without warning, both parts sank out of sight; soon afterwards a steamer hove in sight and passed very near the point where the objects were last seen. Fifteen minutes later, when the ship had gone, the 10 observers saw the objects rise once again from the sea. Now they could see that the upper section was attached to the lower one by a number of shafts or tubes, which were quite bright. Up and down the shafts, small objects 'like beads in a necklace' passed in disorderly fashion. This second display lasted for a few minutes, then the sections closed up, and the whole thing started to sink, eventually disappearing beneath the waves.

One of the witnesses, the wife of another army officer, telephoned the Forte dos Andrades barracks at Guarajá, and the air force base was alerted. An aeroplane was scrambled to investigate, but it arrived on the scene after the objects had disappeared.

'The water was boiling up'

Close encounter of the second kind: Santos, Brazil, 31 October 1963

On 31 October 1963 eight-year-old Rute de Souza was playing near her home in Iguapé, south-west of Santos, when she heard a roaring noise that was growing rapidly louder. Looking round, she saw a silvery object coming down out of the sky, heading towards the nearby Peropava River. After passing over the house the UFO collided with the top of a palm tree and began to twist, turn and wobble in the air. Then Rute saw it fall into the river close to the far bank.

The child turned to run home, and met her mother who, alarmed by the noise, was running towards the river. Then followed Rute's uncle, Raul de Souza, who had been working about 100 yards (90 metres) from the house. The three of them stood transfixed as they watched the surface of the river: at the spot where the object had sunk the water was 'boiling up'. This was followed by an eruption of muddy water, then one of mud.

Rute was not the only witness. On the far bank a number of fishermen had watched the spectacle. One of them, a Japanese gentleman named Tetsuo Ioshigawa, gave descriptions of the incident to official investigators and reporters. The object, shaped like a 'wash basin', was estimated to have been about 25 feet (7.5 metres) in diameter; it had been no more than 20 feet (6 metres) off the ground when it hit the palm tree. The general assumption was that the object was in difficulties after the collision.

The authorities also assumed that a wrecked 'flying saucer' was embedded in the muddy bottom of the river, but divers could find nothing in the 15 feet (5 metres) of water. Finally engineers searched the area with mine detectors, but they too failed to locate the object.

Speculating about the incident in the *Bulletin* of the Aerial Phenomena Research Organisation (APRO), Jim and Coral Lorenzon wrote that the reported size of the UFO suggested it could have carried a crew, and if so, then repairs may have been effected that would have enabled the craft to escape.

Not dreaming and not mad

UFOLOGISTS OFTEN LAMENT the fact that so few UFO sightings are made by people with 'trained minds' – by which they mean scientists and engineers. But this is not really surprising, since the 'trained mind' of a witness is likely to reveal prejudices that discourage him from reporting an extraordinary experience and encourage him to explain it away. On the other hand, unsophisticated observers, unacquainted with the UFO controversy, are often impressive witnesses, telling their story without embroidering it. The sightings of classic 'flying saucers' described here may have more value by virtue of coming from people of little formal education or technical training.

'Dwarf-like creatures with pumpkin-shaped heads'

Close encounter of the third kind: Valensole, France, 1 July 1965

Just after 5 a.m. on 1 July 1965, Maurice Masse, a 41-year-old lavender grower, set to work in his fields situated on the Valensole plateau in the Basses Alpes of south-eastern France. At about 5.45 a.m. he stopped to have a cigarette, parking his tractor by a hillock at the end of a small vineyard that lay along the northern side of the field.

Suddenly he heard a shrill whistling noise and glanced round the hillock, fully expecting to see a helicopter; instead, he saw a dull-coloured object the size of a Renault Dauphine car, shaped like a rugby football, with a cupola on top. It was standing on six metallic legs, and there was also a central support, which appeared to be stuck into the ground. Close to the 'machine' Masse saw two boys, about eight years old, bending over a lavender plant.

Masse crossed the vineyard and approached the boys, believing them to be the 'vandals' who had picked young shoots from a number of his lavender plants on several occasions during the preceding month. Then, to his surprise, he saw that he was not

approaching boys at all, but two dwarf-like creatures with large bald heads. He was about 15 feet (5 metres) from the beings when one of them turned and pointed a pencil-like instrument at him. Immediately he was stopped in his tracks, unable to move any part of his body. (In the first reports of the case it was stated that the witness was 'paralysed', but UFO investigator Aimé Michel suggested the term *immobilised*, perhaps by some form of hypnotic suggestion.)

According to Masse's description, the creatures were less than 4 feet (1.2 metres) tall, and were wearing close-fitting grey-green overalls. They had huge pumpkin-shaped heads, but no hair – only smooth white skin. Their cheeks were wide and fleshy, narrowing to very pointed chins; the eyes were large and slanting. The witness did not mention their noses, but he did describe the mouths, which were like thin slits and opened to form lipless holes. It is rare in close encounters for humanoids to be reported as having their heads uncovered outside the craft, as in this case.

The creatures appeared to communicate

Maurice Masse, owner of vast lavender fields in south-eastern France, stands on the area where a UFO stood while he watched, unable to move. Only weeds grew in this patch of land after the incident

with each other, but not with their mouths, for inarticulate sounds seemed to come from their mid-body regions. The hapless lavender grower thought they were mocking him, although he admitted that their glances were not hostile; indeed, he never had the impression he was face to face with monsters. Masse has never disclosed what took place during the rest of the time he was immobilised, 15 feet (5 metres) from the beings.

After a few minutes the creatures returned to their machine, moving in a remarkable manner: 'falling and rising in space like bubbles in a bottle without apparent support . . . sliding along bands of light . . .' to enter the object through a sliding door. The witness said he could see them looking at him from inside the craft. Suddenly there was a thump from the central support, which retracted, the six legs began to whirl, and the machine floated away at an angle of 45°, making a shrill whistling sound. At 65 feet (20 metres) it just disappeared, although traces of its passage in the direction of Manosque were found on lavender plants for more than 100 yards (90 metres). (These plants withered, then recovered and grew taller and finer than those nearby.)

The farmer grew alarmed as the invisible bonds that held him failed to relax their grip, but after 15 minutes he slowly regained the use of his limbs. He could see marks left by some of the legs of the craft, and almost liquid mud around the hole where the central support had entered the ground. (There had been no rain in the area for several weeks.)

Masse ran down to Valensole, on the outskirts of which is the Café des sports. The proprietor, a friend, was just opening for the day, and Masse, shaken and as white as a sheet, told him part of his story. The café owner pressed Masse for further details of what had happened, but the farmer refused to say any more because he feared the rest of his story would not be believed. His friend advised him to report the incident to the gendarmes, but Masse would not. So the café proprietor rushed to the field, saw the marks and returned to tell Masse's story.

That evening Masse took his 18-year-old daughter to see the landing site; they saw that only four of the craft's legs had left marks on the ground, and that the mud around the central hole had set like concrete.

The world's reaction

Soon after Masse's experience was made public he was questioned by the chief of the local gendarmerie. Crowds of sightseers visited the field, and Valensole was flooded with representatives of the press, radio and television. On 4 July, overwhelmed with interviews and questions, Masse collapsed, seized with an insuperable desire to sleep. Aimé Michel reported that he would have slept 24 hours a day had his wife not awakened him to make him eat.

The initial private investigation was conducted by a local magistrate, who handed his report to *Flying Saucer Review* in October 1965. He said that Masse had prevented his daughter approaching too close to the hole for he feared she might suffer some harmful effect from it; indeed, he was worried about possible genetic effects it might have on himself. In the end he filled the hole, which was shaped like an inverted funnel.

Aimé Michel interviewed the witness twice at Valensole in 1965, and found him anxious and distressed, still worried about possible effects on his health. During his second visit, Michel showed Masse a photograph of a model based on Lonnie Zamora's description of the UFO he had seen at Socorro, New Mexico in the spring of 1964. Masse was staggered that someone should have photographed *his* machine; but when told that it had been seen in the USA by a policeman he sighed with relief: 'You see then that I wasn't dreaming, and that I'm not mad.'

Two years later UFO investigators visited Maurice Masse again and he took them to see the landing site. It was 10 feet (3 metres) in diameter, and distinguishable because lavender plants around the perimeter were withered, and only weeds grew in the inner area – despite the fact that it had been ploughed and replanted.

Although Masse had recovered from his experience, he was anxious to avoid any more publicity. In an endeavour to hide the location of the landing site he trimmed the mass of weeds to the shape of lavender plants. Eventually, he tore up the vineyard, ploughed the lavender field and sowed it all with wheat.

'A disc surrounded with a ring of coloured lights'

Close encounter of the third kind: Puente de Herrera, Valladolid, Spain, 15 August 1970

In 1974 *Flying Saucer Review* received a report from the Charles Fort Group of Valladolid in Spain, who had investigated a UFO sighting that had been made some years earlier. The witness was a 22-year-old woman, a domestic employee in the house of a farmer at Puente de Herrera, close by the river Duero, south of Valladolid. The young woman's name was withheld, at her request, as she had had no primary education, and was illiterate. We shall refer to her simply as the 'señorita'.

On the night of 15 August 1970 the señorita had been watching television when she heard a piercing whistling noise. At the same time the television picture was suddenly blotted out by a mass of lines. Playing with the controls had no effect, so she switched off the set and went to the front door of the house.

The señorita was astounded to see a weird object with various lights standing on the drive. And nearby there stood a very strange-looking 'man' who seemed to be surveying a crop of alfalfa in an adjacent field. Very scared, the young woman went back inside the house and shut the door. Then the whistling sound began again but, when she went to look out of the window of her room, both machine and 'man' had gone.

The señorita told only her boyfriend of her experience at the time. Members of her family became aware of it only in March 1972 when, after her brother-in-law had made some observation about UFOs, she told them about what she had seen. It was her brother-in-law who passed the information to the Charles Fort Group.

During the investigation that followed, J. Macías and his fellow researchers learned that the period of time between the onset of the whistling noise and the witness first looking out of the window was about 5 minutes. The whistling noise persisted while she was peering through the door, but seemed a little less intense. She had switched off the porch lights as she usually did between 10.30 and 11.00 p.m., so she felt nobody could have seen her when she opened the door.

The UFO, which was balanced on several 'feet' on the road surface, was about 12 feet (4 metres) wide and 8 feet (2.5 metres) high. The upper part consisted of a hemispherical cupola, which seemed to be made of crystal. On top of this a bluish-white light revolved erratically, the light dimming whenever it slowed down. The cupola was supported by a disc surrounded with a ring of coloured lights that changed constantly from white to purple and then yellow.

The occupant of the craft was about 5 feet 10 inches (1.8 metres) tall and was dressed in a dark, tight-fitting garment and a helmet. Around his ankles and wrists there were glowing white 'bracelets' and in the middle of his belt was a square 'buckle' of similar iridescent material. The señorita was not sure about the colour of his skin, and could not see any hair. She said the 'man' seemed to be interested in the alfalfa, and walked towards it with unusually long strides.

A persistent afterglow

According to the witness, physical vestiges of the craft were left at the landing site, for when she went to the window of her room she saw a soft glow where the object had been standing. Intrigued by this, she inspected the ground. On the surface of the road there were black footprints, similar to those made by ordinary shoes, the heel mark narrower than that of the sole. The marks must have been seen by everybody coming to the house, but the señorita told no one of her experience at the time and therefore did not draw attention to them. While they remained, however, the area where the UFO had landed continued to glow at night.

The investigators considered that the señorita's illiteracy added to the authenticity of her account on the grounds that she could hardly have fabricated a story of such complexity. After speaking with members of her family they realised that their knowledge of other UFO encounters was insufficient for her to have picked up such detailed data from them. Furthermore, there seemed to be no motivation for a hoax, for it was only by chance that she mentioned her experience to her brother-in-law 18 months after the event. Other members of the family later told the investigators that after their first interview with the señorita she had wept hysterically and rounded on her brother-in-law for having given away her secret.

UFOs can kill

EVER SINCE the post-war wave of UFO sightings began, a debate has raged among ufologists as to whether or not the objects seen in the sky are hostile.

Some researchers cling to the belief that a surveillance of this planet is being carried out by extra-terrestrial explorers. Others take this a step further and proclaim that 'space beings' come to the Earth to warn Man of the evil of his ways. Yet others believe that the extra-terrestrials – or meta-terrestrials, if one holds the theory that they are denizens of 'parallel universes' – are engaged in a struggle for possession of the human race, and that they have no interest in human welfare.

Still other investigators claim that UFOs are psychically caused phenomena, while others counter by suggesting that UFOs may cause manifestations of psychic phenomena. Lastly, there are those who have come to the conclusion that UFOs are mere products of the witnesses' imaginations.

On the whole, however, UFO researchers assume that they are dealing with a benign phenomenon. If human beings occasionally suffer harm from UFOs, they believe, it is either an unintended consequence of UFO activity that had no malicious purpose, or it was a purely defensive response.

In the cases discussed here, human witnesses of UFOs suffered temporary or permanent injury – and in one case, death. In two of them the injured people could be held guilty of provoking the trouble. Nonetheless, these incidents invoke the spectre first raised by H. G. Wells in *War of the worlds* – of attack on mankind by alien beings.

'An eerie orange light'

Close encounter of the second kind: São Vicente, São Paulo, Brazil, 4 November 1957

The Brazilian coastal fort of Itaipu is situated at São Vicente, close to the port of Santos in the state of São Paulo. To the two sentries patrolling the gun emplacements in the small hours of 4 November 1957, everything seemed quiet. Nothing warned them that within a few minutes they were to be put through a nightmarish ordeal that still lacks an explanation.

At 2 a.m. the sentries spotted a 'bright star' that suddenly appeared above the horizon over the Atlantic. It grew larger and the soldiers realised that it was approaching them at high speed. They were astonished by this glowing object, which they thought was an aeroplane, but they gave no thought to sounding the alarm.

In a few seconds the UFO, travelling silently, reached a point high above the fort and halted. Then it floated down until it had stopped motionless some 150 feet (50 metres) above the highest gun turret, bathing the ground between the turrets with an eerie orange light. The object appeared to be circular and was, in the soldiers' words, about the size of a 'big Douglas' (meaning, presumably, a Douglas DC-6). The sentries could now hear a gentle humming noise that seemed to be associated with it.

Without warning, a wave of searing heat suddenly engulfed the men. Fire seemed to be burning all over their uniforms, while the humming intensified.

One sentry staggered, dazed, and then fell unconscious to the ground. His comrade managed to stumble into a relatively sheltered spot beneath one of the guns. But once there his mind seemed to give way: he was seized by horror and rent the air with bloodcurdling screams.

His terrible cries awakened the rest of the garrison, but within seconds the power supply cut off, lights went out and equipment failed. An officer tried to start the emergency generator, but that too failed. Meanwhile, the horrifying screams continued and confusion turned to panic in the dark subterranean corridors.

Suddenly, the lights returned. The officers and men who were first to get into the open were in time to see a great orange light climbing away vertically, before shooting off at high speed. The last of the soldiers to arrive found those who had preceded them examining the unconscious sentry while the other was still crouched in hiding and crying hysterically.

In the sick bay both men were found to have 'first- and deep second-degree burns – mostly on areas that had been protected by clothes'. The sentry who had retained consciousness was in deep nervous shock and many hours were to pass before he could talk.

The fort's electric clocks had stopped at 2.03 a.m., which suggested that the whole nightmare experience had lasted no more than about four minutes.

Later that morning the colonel in command of Fort Itaipu issued orders forbidding the communication of the incident to anyone. Intelligence officers were quickly at work conducting an investigation, and a report was sent to army headquarters. Some days later officers from the US military mission arrived, together with Brazilian Air Force officers. Meanwhile, the sentries were flown to Rio de Janeiro and admitted to the Army Central Hospital, where a security net was promptly drawn around them.

Three weeks later, an officer from the fort who was interested in UFO reports sought out Dr Olavo Fontes, who was involved in the investigation of the famous Antônio Villas Boas case examined earlier. The officer had been present at the fort during the incident and, once he was satisfied that his name would never be divulged, he gave Fontes full details of the case. Dr Fontes approached medical colleagues at the hospital, who confirmed that two soldiers were being treated for severe burns, but would tell him nothing more about their case.

Without further corroboration, Dr Fontes could not publish an account. So the case lingered in the files until mid 1959, when, by chance, the doctor met three other officers who in the course of conversation confirmed what had happened. Thanks to the unauthorised disclosures of the officers who talked to Dr Fontes, the world has some knowledge, tantalisingly incomplete though it is, of a UFO's unwelcome visit to Fort Itaipu on that terrifying night.

'Like an upturned wash basin'

Close encounter of the third kind: Pilar de Goiás, Brazil, 13 August 1967

Illiterate, simple, honest, trustworthy and reserved – this was how Inácio de Souza, a 41-year-old Brazilian ranch worker, was described by his employer. He was to meet a tragic end, apparently as a result of an encounter with a UFO in which, gripped by fear, he resorted to violence, and was repaid in kind.

On 13 August 1967, at about 4 p.m., de Souza and his wife Luiza, the parents of five children, were returning to the ranch after a shopping trip on foot to the nearest village. The ranch was near Pilar de Goiás, some 150 miles (240 kilometres) from Brasilia, the country's capital. The couple had almost reached the first building on the ranch when they saw three 'people' apparently playing on the landing strip. (The ranch owner, a well-known and extremely wealthy man, possessed several aircraft.) De Souza thought the trespassers were naked, but his wife said they were wearing skin-tight yellow clothes. At the same time the intruders seemed to see the couple, and started to approach them.

It was then that de Souza spotted a strange aircraft at the end of the runway. It was either on or just above the ground, and looked like an upturned wash basin. The ranch hand suddenly became very frightened, unslung his .44 carbine, took aim and fired a shot at the nearest figure.

Almost immediately a beam of green light was emitted by the strange craft. It hit de Souza on the head and shoulder, and he fell to the ground. As his wife ran to his assistance she saw the three 'persons' enter the craft, which thereupon took off vertically at high speed, and with a noise like the humming of bees.

During the following few days, de Souza complained of numbness and tingling of the body, of headaches, and of severe nausea. On the third day he developed continuous tremors of the hands and head. The rancher was informed of the incident on that day, and he flew his sick employee to Goiânia, more than 180 miles (300 kilometres) away, where he was examined by a doctor.

'Burns' were discovered on his head and trunk, in the shape of perfect circles 6 inches (15 centimetres) across. The doctor thought they could be a rash produced by a poisonous plant. When he laboured this theory the rancher told him de Souza's story of the encounter with the UFO and its occupants. The surprised doctor proposed some tests of de Souza's faeces, urine and blood, prescribed an unguent for the 'burns' and expressed his opinion that de Souza had suffered an hallucination and that he had already contracted some disease. He made no secret of the fact that he had no time for flying saucer stories, that he did not believe de Souza and that the whole affair should be hushed up.

The sick man and his employer stayed on in Goiânia for five days while investigation and treatment continued. When de Souza was discharged the illness had been diagnosed as leukaemia. The prognosis was poor: he was expected to live no more than 60 days. And he did indeed waste away quickly, covered with white and yellowish-white blotches. He died on 11 October 1967.

Did alien action kill the ranch worker? The doctor in Goiânia might have wished to suppress de Souza's story because he feared the panic that such a disturbing tale could cause. This could have been the motive behind his 'hallucination' theory, which will not bear much examination. If de Souza did have an hallucination, then his wife shared it – unless she dutifully lied about her experience out of loyalty to him. And if there was a joint hallucination, then there must have been some agency responsible for causing it – an agency whose nature is as mysterious as the strange 'aircraft' and 'people' that the couple thought they saw.

'It's blinded me!'

Close encounter of the second kind: Itatiánia, Rio de Janeiro, Brazil, 30 August 1970

Brazil seems to have had more than its share of UFO incidents in which witnesses have suffered injury or even death. Only a few years after Inácio de Souza's disastrous experience, another Brazilian came to harm in a brief and terrifying encounter with a mysterious object. The victim on this occasion was Almiro Martins de Freitas, a security watchman who was on duty at the time.

The incident occurred at 9.30 p.m. on 30 August 1970. De Freitas, a married man with three children, was working for the Special Internal Security Patrol Service on the Funil Dam at Itatiánia, in the state of Rio de Janeiro. On this evening he was out on patrol, inspecting the area for which he was responsible. Heavy rain had just fallen and the ground was wet. He had almost come to the end of his beat when he saw a hump-shaped mass on a mound, displaying a row of multicoloured lights. Orange, red and blue were among the colours of the light that the object was emitting.

De Freitas felt uneasy but he overcame his first instinctive urge to retreat as fast as possible. He began to move cautiously towards the object. Even when he had come to a distance of about 50 feet (15 metres) from the object, its shape was still unclear to him in the darkness.

At this point an intense noise assailed his ears. It was like the sound of a jet engine, and it deafened him. Startled, he drew his revolver and started firing towards the lights. After his second shot there was a dazzling flash from the object, seemingly aimed at the security guard. De Freitas was blinded. He fired a third shot wildly, and then a wave of heat engulfed him. He found that he was immobilised.

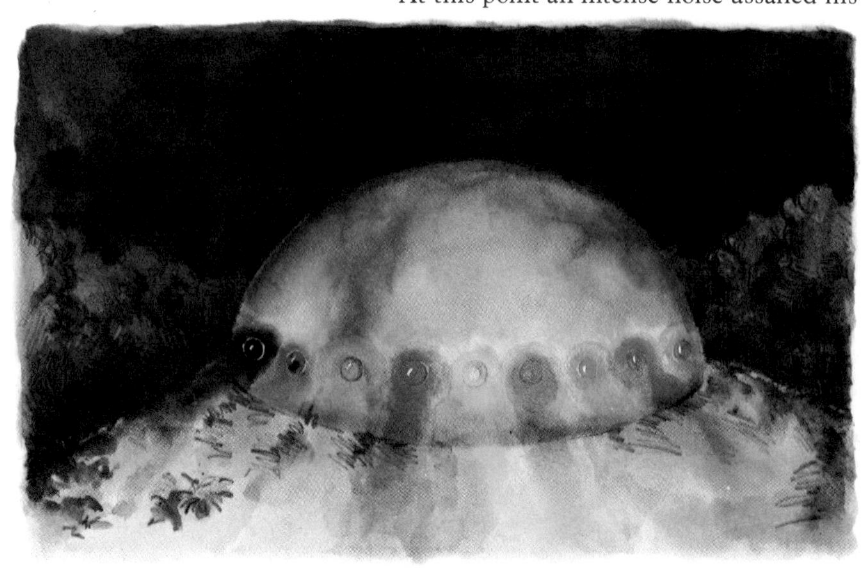

Shortly afterwards another watchman and a passing motorist arrived at the spot. They found a surreal scene. De Freitas was standing stiffly by a mound of earth, brandishing his revolver and shouting warnings to them: 'Don't look! Beware the flash! It's blinded me!' The two newcomers contrived to carry the stricken man to the car. After a while he began to recover his ability to move, but he did not recover his sight.

A significant fact supporting de Freitas's account was noticed at the scene of the incident. At the place where he had seen the multicoloured lights there was a circular area of dry ground, despite the downpour that had soaked the ground elsewhere.

From Itatiánia the security guard was taken to a hospital in the city of Guanabara, where psychiatrists and ophthalmologists subjected him to psychological and physical examination. These tests showed that, physiologically, the patient was perfectly normal. His blindness, the investigators decided, had been brought about by shock. De Freitas became noticeably disturbed whenever he talked about the experience.

On 3 September the incident found its way into a number of Brazilian newspapers. At the time of these reports, although a full three days had elapsed, de Freitas had still not recovered his vision.

From this point the investigations were taken over by the government's security authorities, with a major role being played by the department assigned to study UFOs. Civilian UFO researchers who attempted to find out more about the case found that the official investigation was being handled with an air of secrecy. Evidently the Brazilian government took seriously this latest incident in the string of violent events involving UFOs intruding into its national territory.

Sick with fear

ONE OF THE MORE CURIOUS aspects of the UFO phenomenon is the way in which certain individuals are sometimes singled out for more than one visitation. A notorious example is the astronomer George Adamski; another, more credible, is the experience of Maureen Puddy of Victoria, Australia, who had two close encounters in three weeks in July 1952. Our first story concerns another such 'repeater', who experienced UFO sightings and related phenomena for nearly 20 years, culminating in a terrifying encounter on a lonely road in southern France.

Our second story is a close encounter of the second kind – with a difference. In addition to the interference with electrical equipment that has come to be regarded as normal in UFO sightings, there were some more unusual side effects: after the sighting, the witness noticed that the front of her car, which had been dirty, was as clean as if it had just been washed, and her hair, which had recently been treated with a permanent wave, went completely straight!

'Blinded by the fierce light'

Close encounter of the second kind: Noé, Haut-Garonne, France, 29 August 1975

It was 10.45 p.m. on 29 August 1975 and Monsieur R. Cyrus – a former gendarme turned businessman, aged 48 – was driving along departmental route D10 from Longages to a point south of Noé where the road joins Route Nationale 125. It is a country district, deep in the Haut-Garonne department of south-western France. The sky was clear, the weather was mild, and a light south-east wind was blowing. Under a bright Moon, he had travelled about three-quarters of the way along the road when he observed, in a field to the right of the road, an aluminium-coloured machine. When, a second or two later, the car was almost level with this object, the underpart became illuminated with a phosphorescent glow, and it floated in the air, at bonnet height, towards the front of the car.

M. Cyrus rammed on the brakes just as the object tilted back to present its underside to the driver. At that moment the luminosity increased enormously and, blinded by the fierce light, M. Cyrus threw up his arms to protect his head and eyes. His car swerved off the road and ended up in a shallow ditch. Even as that happened the UFO shot straight up and hovered, a bright point of light in the sky, directly above the car. All this took place in the space of five seconds or so, and there was no sound whatever from the UFO.

M. Cyrus sat motionless, getting out of his car only when, about a minute later, a passing motorist stopped nearby and came over to open the door for him. 'I thought your car was exploding,' he said.

The former gendarme stood shocked and unsteady, touching himself 'to see if he were still alive'. Then he muttered: 'Good heavens – is this it?'

Meanwhile the light of the UFO, high above, was fluctuating in intensity, and had taken on a reddish tinge. M. Cyrus stood where he was, watching the phenomenon for some 15 minutes. A compact beam shone down from the object, illuminating the car but

not the surrounding area.

By now a number of people had arrived on the scene, and the consensus of opinion was that M. Cyrus should report the matter immediately to the gendarmerie, but he declared – something that puzzled him later – 'You all know me; I'll go to the gendarmerie tomorrow. Now I'm off home!' His wife said that when he arrived home he was distraught.

When questioned later the witness said he could not recall having been 'paralysed' by the UFO's presence, but he did remember that his throat was all 'jammed up', and he was unable to utter a sound until the other motorist opened the door. There were other physiological effects: after the encounter, the witness experienced bouts of sleepiness, even when driving; whenever he stopped doing anything he found himself falling asleep. His eyesight, too, was briefly affected: when awakening on the two mornings following his experience, he had black spots before the eyes, but these gradually faded.

Surprisingly, there were no signs of burns or scratches, or changes of colour on the car after the event. There was another unusual feature about the sighting: the engine did not stall during the event, and the lights continued to work normally throughout.

Attempts were made by investigators to locate landing marks or other traces of the UFO, but nothing was found. Aerial photographs also failed to reveal anything.

It was unfortunate that, although the motorist who approached M. Cyrus after the sighting presumably made a report to the gendarmes, and spoke to the investigators, he declined to make a statement, and refused to allow his name to be mentioned. There were two other independent but vague reports of lights in the sky, and of one in a field some distance from the road.

During the course of their investigation for the French UFO organisation *Lumières dans la nuit*, the researchers – a M. Cattiau and his colleagues – greatly assisted by the good-natured collaboration of M. Cyrus, unearthed the remarkable fact that M. Cyrus appeared to be one of the group of witnesses known as 'repeaters': he had had at least three earlier UFO experiences.

In 1957 he was at a vineyard at Quillan in Aude during the grape harvest, when he saw, at about 8.30 one evening, two orange-coloured, cigar-shaped objects some 200 yards (180 metres) away. They were hovering over rows of vines while a cart passed below, its driver apparently oblivious to what was happening. M. Cyrus called other vineyard workers from their dinner who, when they saw the intruders, began to run towards them, whereupon the objects departed silently.

Again, near midnight one day in the autumn of 1974, M. Cyrus was driving with his wife from Noé to Muret when they saw a strange object to their left looking like flashes of light. These were suddenly succeeded by a huge orange sphere that illuminated the countryside, and kept pace with their car for about 5 miles (8 kilometres). When they arrived at the village of Ox they were able to compare the size of the sphere with that of the church, and the sphere appeared enormous. Then, as they passed, a nearby transformer appeared to explode; it was confirmed next day that the circuit breaker had tripped during the night for some unknown reason.

Twice in 1975, a few weeks before the encounter of 29 August, M. Cyrus stated that he had heard guttural voices speaking in an unidentifiable language on his car radio – each time when he had the radio switched off! While this is not strictly within the UFO realm, one is forced to wonder whether or not M. Cyrus is a deep-trance subject, or perhaps possesses a degree of clairvoyance – in which case something could well have been 'beamed in' on him, setting him up for the big encounter of 29 August. It would answer many a question if we knew *why*.

'Glowing orange and silver'

Close encounter of the second kind: Launceston, Tasmania, Australia, 22 September 1974

Late on the afternoon of 22 September 1974 a woman who wishes to be known only as Mrs W. arrived at the junction of the Diddleum and Tayene Plains roads, around 30 miles (50 kilometres) north-east of Launceston, Tasmania, Australia. It was raining, and the mountains were shrouded in mist, as she parked her car around 200 yards (180 metres) from the junction and waited for the arrival of the relative she was due to pick up. Because there was a steep bank to the left of the road, she parked her car on the other side to ensure that any of the heavy log trucks that frequently used the narrow road would see the vehicle clearly.

Over the car radio, she heard that the time was 5.20 p.m. Suddenly the radio developed a high-pitched whine and the whole landscape lit up, the bright light flooding the inside of the car. She leaned over to switch off the radio – and, looking up through the windscreen, saw a glowing orange and silver object moving between two trees and coming downhill towards her. It was about the size of a large car, moving slowly 50 to 60 feet (15 to 18 metres) above the ground, and dropping steadily towards the road.

Not surprisingly, Mrs W. panicked. She started the car and began to reverse up the road, away from the UFO. The object went on approaching until it was at the level of the fence at the side of the road, and hovered over the middle of the road about 30 to 35 yards (25 to 30 metres) from Mrs W.'s car. It was domed on top, although it was difficult to make out its shape because of the intense orange-yellow light it emitted; Mrs W. could not estimate its size. Beneath the dome, the UFO was silver-grey in colour. There was a wide band on which there could have been portholes, and six to eight horizontal bands below it, decreasing in diameter; their width was about 5 feet (1.5 metres) in all. At the bottom of the object was a small revolving disc, and below this what appeared to be a box or tube, which protruded from the base a short way.

After reversing about 100 yards (90 metres), Mrs W. accidentally backed the car over the edge of the road, and the wheels stuck fast. The UFO now stopped in front of the witness. It then dipped to the right and moved away to the south-west over a valley beside the road. It then rose vertically upwards, fairly fast, and was lost from Mrs W.'s field of vision. The entire sighting had lasted 3 to 4 minutes.

Mrs W. jumped out of her car and ran all the way to her house, which was about a mile (1.6 kilometres) away. She had the feeling that she was being watched, and kept looking up to see if the UFO was following her; she did not, however, see anything. When she arrived home, her husband and son went out to inspect the car. They could see nothing unusual.

The next day, however, when the car was towed home, it was noticed that the front of the car was exceptionally clean, although the rest of it was as dirty as it had been before the encounter. Previously, there had been cat footprints all over the bonnet – and yet this part of the car was as clean as if it had been given a good polish. Neither Mrs W. nor her husband believed that the rain of the previous day could have cleaned the front of the car while leaving the back dirty.

For some days after her terrifying experience, Mrs W. was ill with nervous tension – a kind of state of shock. Her hair, which had been newly treated with a permanent wave, turned straight after her encounter.

Mr and Mrs W. claimed that the car radio was in perfect working order before the UFO sighting; afterwards, it was reported that it suffered from distortion. This, of course, is a common phenomenon in close encounters with UFOs.

Mrs W. initially reported the sighting to the Royal Australian Air Force (RAAF), who could not supply any explanation – they ruled out such things as weather balloons, aircraft, helicopters and meteorological phenomena. The case was investigated by the northern representative of the Tasmanian UFO Investigation Centre, and subsequently reported to *Flying Saucer Review* by W.K. Roberts.

A UFO comes to town

PHOTOGRAPHS OUGHT TO BE good evidence of a UFO sighting, but they are not always so. Sometimes, for example, a UFO can appear on a picture when the photographer did not actually see one. Sometimes, too, the object appears different on the photograph from the way that the observer remembers seeing it. So the evidence from even genuine pictures is often ambiguous.

In this case, the photographer remembered the UFO as different from the picture. And, after all, if the UFO was in such a highly populated area as south London, why was there only one witness?

'Strange shadow effects'

Close encounter of the first kind: Streatham, London, 15 December 1966

Sightings of true UFOs over London are a rarity. Many reports are made, but these often prove to be misidentifications of lights in the sky. This is hardly surprising considering the great volume of aircraft flying over the city on the way in or out of Heathrow airport. There are also many other aircraft flying over at great height and, at night, satellites that reflect the rays of a Sun already well below the western horizon. Few who report sightings in fact fulfil the condition of having seen a UFO at close range – near enough to be classified as a close encounter of the first kind.

One sighting towards the end of 1966, however, may have fulfilled this condition – and the report was reinforced by photographs. These photographs seem to show remarkable changes in the shape of the images, and the changes cannot be due entirely to changes of aspect of the photographed object.

The day of the sighting was Thursday, 15 December 1966. It was one of the shortest days of the year: the Sun set at 3.53 p.m. The weather was unpleasant – misty, dull and damp, with drizzle, rain and low cloud – and maximum visibility was 2 miles (3 kilometres).

At approximately 2.30 that afternoon, Anthony Russell was standing by the open window of his flat in Lewin Road, Streatham, south-west London. Lewin Road is at the southern end of Streatham High Road and just west of Streatham Common. The window by which Russell stood faces approximately north-north-west. A keen photographer, he was testing for resolution two new 2 × converters for his Zenith 3N single lens reflex camera (focal length 135 millimetres increased to 270 millimetres by one converter). During the testing, Russell was aiming the camera at the gable of a house on the far side of Lewin Road, about 28 yards (26 metres) from the lens. The camera was loaded with 35-millimetre Gratispool colour film.

Suddenly Russell became aware of an

This is the first photograph taken by Anthony Russell of a UFO that he sighted from his flat window. There is a hint of an efflux from the base of the object on the right. The bar seen on the gable of the house across the road supports a chimney that is off camera

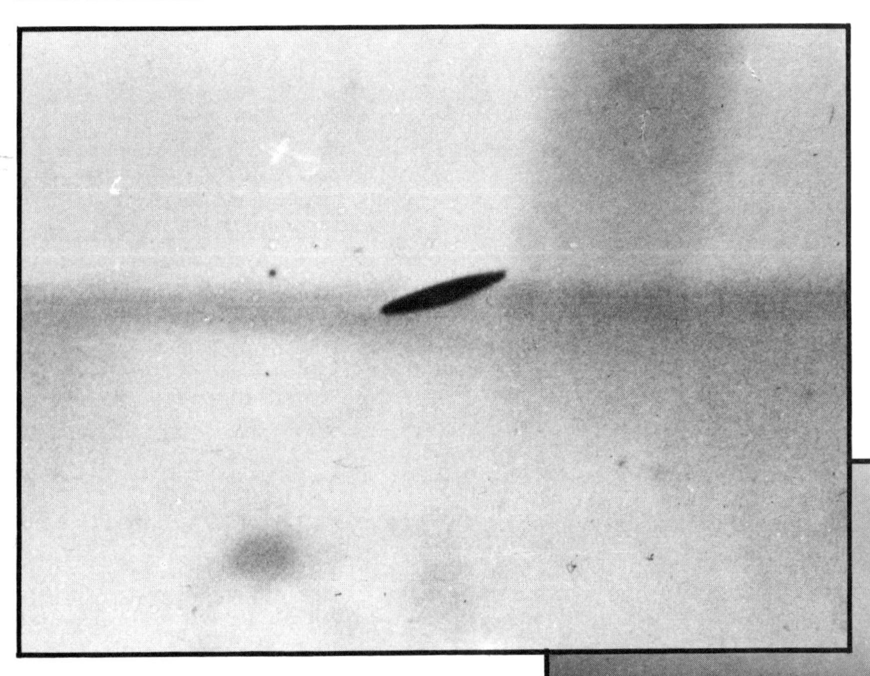

well. A fourth – the last to be taken – revealed a dim shape that had little definition. Russell was puzzled by the object's apparent changes of shape because he did not recall seeing such changes. He recalled seeing only changes of aspect of the UFO.

It is reasonable to assume that the eight blank frames were due to the speedy rolling on of the film between shots in the witness's excitement, occasioned by an incident that lasted two minutes at most. Here is a reconstruction of those two minutes:

After the initial swift descent and abrupt halt of the UFO, Russell took his first two shots. He used the single converter that he

object in the sky falling suddenly, stopping dead, and then drifting slowly earthwards with a pendulum-like motion. Amazed at first, but rapidly collecting his wits about him, he 'slapped the camera to infinity' and began snapping. He thought he got 12 photographs. The last two shots were taken as the object moved away, at first slowly and then at much greater speed.

The witness had had limited contact with UFO literature before in as much as his father had designed a cover for the book *Flying saucers have landed* (1953) by George Adamski and Desmond Leslie. Russell did not think much of the book and, after meeting Adamski, thought even less of the subject. But his scepticism received a jolt as he stood photographing the strange object in the sky.

Russell left the rest of the film in the camera so that he could take photographs at Christmas and sent it away for processing after the holiday period. In the meantime he told a few friends what had happened. They were inclined to laugh off the incident, but he felt it was worth investigating. He did not wish for the publicity a newspaper might have brought him, but he was not sure who would be genuinely interested. Fearing he would get short shrift from established bodies such as the Royal Astronomical Society or the Royal Aeronautical Society, he looked through the telephone directory under the word 'flying' and so happened on *Flying Saucer Review*. He wrote to the magazine, explaining what he expected to be found on his pictures when the film was returned, and the magazine arranged for R.H.B. Winder, an engineer, and Gordon Creighton to help in an investigation once the pictures were available for study.

From the start of the investigation there was a measure of disappointment for the witness, for only 3 of the 12 frames came out

Top: the second photograph shows the UFO edge-on, which emphasises its disc shape. The expert who examined the photographs for fraud could not explain the strange shadow effects on this shot

Above: the third photograph caught the UFO in a slanted position, perhaps in the ascent since it was taken just before the object sped away. When enlarged, the picture revealed a marked efflux to the left

had been testing, set at 1/125 second (f/5.6). He then hurried away from the window and fitted the second (Panagar) converter. With a focal length now of 540 millimetres, he set the exposure at 1/25 second (f/11). Returning to the window, he saw the object 'stand on end' and present its full circular shape to him before turning through 90° about a vertical axis until it was edge on. The UFO then started to move to his right. During all that period, Russell shot only two successful snaps, though he could not have known this at the time. It was during the moment of movement to the right that the third good picture was captured. Then the fourth followed as the UFO accelerated away. By the time Russell reset the camera for the next shot, the object had gone.

After investigation, the researchers handed the transparencies to *Flying Saucer Review*'s photographic consultant, Percy Hennell. After examining them he made plate negatives from the first three. He stated that they were 'genuine photographs of an object in the air, and, in the case of the first, some distance beyond the house opposite the position where the photographer stood'. He could detect no signs of the transparencies

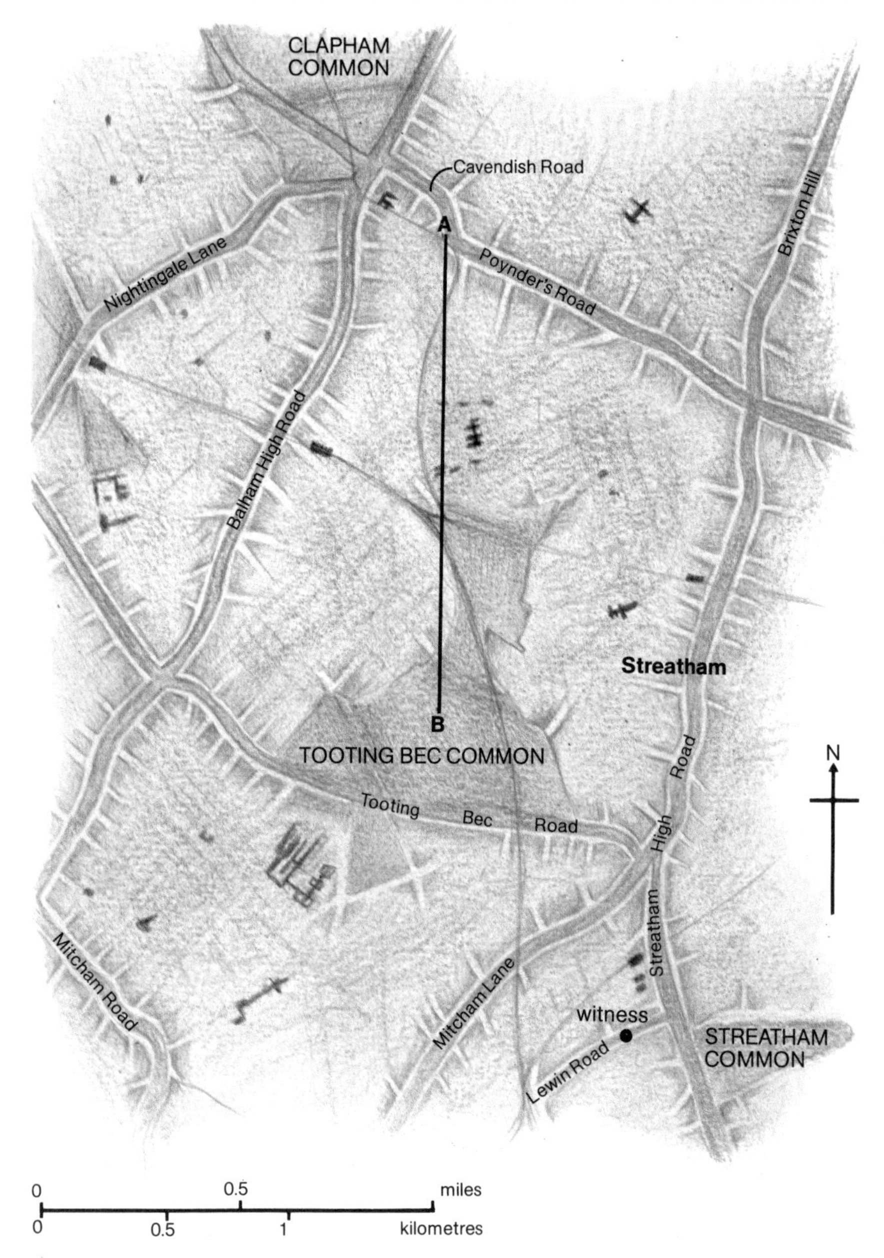

having been tampered with. Later the transparencies were projected onto a 12-foot (3.5-metre) square screen. Close inspection revealed nothing untoward.

The investigators ascertained that the object was not luminous, and that it was virtually impossible for the witness to distinguish any colour owing to the fact that it was being viewed as a dark object against a light background. Russell merely suggested it might have been maroon.

The first photograph shows the gable of the house opposite Russell's flat with a near-horizontal bar to the right that acts as a support for a chimney that is off camera. Winder estimated that the bar would have been at an angle of elevation of 10° from the lens of the camera. Russell thought the object might have been anything up to a mile (1.6 kilometres) away. In the photograph there is a hint of an efflux streaming to the right from the base of the UFO – a feature more clearly seen when the image had been enlarged and viewed on a projector.

Winder pointed out that the silhouetted image of the UFO on the first photograph bore a remarkable similarity to the shape drawn by Police Constable Colin Perks after his sighting of a UFO at Wilmslow, Cheshire, on 7 January 1966, at 4.10 a.m. Constable Perks was checking the back door of a shop when he heard a high-pitched whine. He turned and looked over the car park behind the shops, which was east. There he saw a solid-looking object – stationary – some 35 feet (10 metres) above the grass of the meadow beyond the car park. It was about 100 yards (90 metres) from him. Perks said the UFO's upper surfaces glowed steadily with a greenish-grey colour, a glow that did not hide the definite shape of the object. He said the lines in his sketch 'represented rounded, but fairly sharp changes in the profile, matched by shading in the glow'. Nowhere could he see openings like portholes or doors. His estimate of a diameter of 30 feet (9 metres) for the base was based on a mental comparison with a 30-foot (9-metre) long bus. After about five seconds the object moved off east-south-east with no change of sound. Then it disappeared.

Russell's other photographs brought no further comparisons to mind. In the second picture there are strange shadow effects, particularly one that slants away in the '7 o'clock' position. Hennell could offer no explanation for this.

The third photograph seems to have been blurred either by the motion of the object – it was beginning to move away – or by camera shake. An efflux effect is also noticeable to the left of the object. This in fact was quite pronounced when the picture was enlarged.

Judging from Russell's position and the 2-mile (3-kilometre) visibility limit, the object appears to have been somewhere on a line from the sighting point via Tooting Bec Common to Cavendish Road.

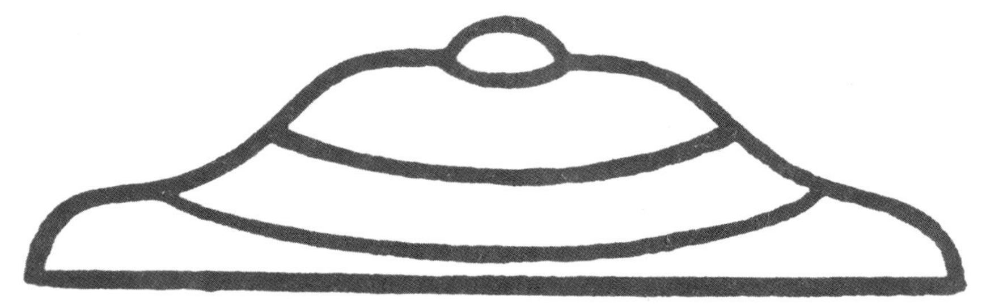

Top: map of the area in which Russell spotted the UFO over Streatham. The object appears to have been somewhere along line A–B

Above: a drawing made by PC Colin Perks of the UFO he saw in Cheshire about a year before Russell's sighting. The two reports were strikingly similar

A contact at Heathrow airport told the investigators that the object was not observed on the radar screens, but it is possible that it missed the radar sweep by virtue of its plummeting fall in between sweeps.

The Ministry of Defence (Air) was asked about weather balloons on 15 December 1966. The answer was that four were released in south and south-west England earlier than the sighting, but that they would not have migrated to the London area.